GW00457991

EXCEL
SHORTCUTS
NINJA

HENRY E. MEJIA

EXCEL SHORTCUTS NINJA

Copyright © 2020 HENRY E. MEJIA

All rights reserved. No part of this publication may be reproduced, stored in any data retrieval system or transmitted in any form or by any electronic, mechanical, photocopying, recording or other means, without the prior written permission of the author, except in the case of brief reviews used in literary reviews and certain non-commercial uses provided by the Copyright Law.

DEDICATION

To my parents, who have taught me that life is about
overcoming obstacles and enjoying it.

CONTENTS

ACKNOWLEDGMENTS

I would like to thank all those who supported me throughout the creation of this book, either with words of encouragement or with ideas to improve it.

INTRODUCTION

Welcome to a new EXCEL NINJA book! The fastest, the most practice-based and definitely the most straightforward Excel Book Series you will ever find!

You will learn to use with confidence the most important and useful Excel SHORTCUTS.

Excel Ninja Series is all about this:

- **Learning fast**
- **Having fun while learning**
- **Learning trough practice (from the very beginning)**
- **No unnecessary fillers to make the book look longer**

- **The most straightforward and lean approach**
- **Getting results!**

Loaded with a gigantic amount of practice spreadsheets, examples, and recommendations.

My goal for this Excel Ninja Series was to achieve the perfect balance between a lot of exercises and examples without compromising the straightforward approach, and that's what you will find here!

That being said, I would like to summarize the benefits of becoming an Excel SHORTCUTS Ninja:

- Increased chances of getting a promotion and better jobs (Because you are more productive and have better skills)
- Less workload (Excel does the heavy lifting)
- More free time
- Less stress

- A sense of growth (When you learn something new you feel great, and you know it!)
- Etc., etc.

I could spend more time, word and pages explaining to you the benefits and the importance of becoming an EXCEL SHORTCUTS NINJA, but I promised that I won't fill this book with unnecessary words so let's start the first chapter right now!

GET YOUR 31 PRACTICE SPREADSHEETS (.XLSX)

Before starting Chapter 1 I recommend you to get your 31 practice spreadsheets. Those exercise files are included for everyone who purchases this book. They will serve you at the end of each chapter to reinforce what you have learned and make sure you have learned it well.

To get them immediately just **Scan this QR Code** or go directly to **https://bit.ly/hemejia2** and follow the instructions.

If for any reason both the QR Code and the Link don't work, send an email to ems.online.empire@gmail.com saying:

"Hello, I bought your book EXCEL SHORTCUTS NINJA and I need the 31 practice spreadsheets"

I will gladly reply to you but you may need to wait a few business days.

Now you are ready to start Chapter 1. Let's go!

CHAPTER 1:

CATEGORIES OF SHORTCUTS AND BOOK LAYOUT

WHAT IS A SHORTCUT?

A SHORTCUT is a combination of key strokes (in your keyboard) that perform a specific action in your computer. They are also known as "Hotkeys" or "Keyboard Shortcuts". Normally, those actions are performed using the mouse trough the Excel spreadsheets and clicking the features in the upper part of Excel (Ribbon).

The main benefit of using Excel Shortcuts is the speed. You will notice that when you go through the exercises of this book, you will be able to work in Excel at a higher speed.

Let me explain the "speed" argument with the most basic example. Imagine that you need to Copy something in your spreadsheet "Sales" and you need to Paste it at the bottom of the database in the spreadsheet called "Management", the process would look like this:

OPTION 1 (WITHOUT SHORTCUTS):

- Grab your mouse, and right click on the cell
- Select copy
- Click on the spreadsheet "Management"
- Scroll down to the bottom of the database
- Right click
- Select Paste

OPTION 1 (WITH SHORTCUTS):

- Shortcut for copying
- Shortcut for changing the spreadsheet

- Shortcut to go to the bottom of the database
- Shortcut to paste

Although it might seem like no difference in time, the Option 1 would take like 8 seconds (depending on the size of the database) while the Option 2 would take like 3 seconds (and it doesn't matter the size of the database)

So, we can say that Shortcuts could easily cut your routine worktime in Excel by half!

WHICH ARE THE SHORTCUTS CATEGORIES?

There are no official categories for Shortcuts, but they can be divided in:

- Formatting Shortcuts
- Movement shortcuts
- Inserting/Filling Shortcuts

- Grid Shortcuts
- View Shortcuts

I use those words so you can get an idea of what the shortcuts can do for you.

Nevertheless, I have divided the shortcuts by levels, and that is how you are going to learn to use them. Each level has shortcuts from different categories, but the most important thing to consider is that each level is organized by difficulty, time saving potential and frequency of use.

LEVEL 0 SHORTCUTS

These shortcuts are the ones that every Windows or Mac user needs to know, even if they don't use Excel. Knowing how to correctly use these basic shortcuts will save lots of time.

LEVEL 1 SHORTCUTS

These shortcuts are the basic Excel shortcuts. You can't call yourself an Excel Ninja without knowing all of these.

LEVEL 2 SHORTCUTS

These level 2 is the Holy Grail of the fast Excel users. You will get most of your time saved by Shortcuts in this level. The frequency of use is very high and the time that they save is gigantic.

LEVEL 3 SHORTCUTS

The level 3 is a little bit more advanced. These shortcuts can save you a lot of time although they are not as frequently used as the level 2 shortcuts.

NOTE: Each level builds upon each other, so please DO NOT try to go straight for level 2 or 3. You will need to learn them in the right order.

That's how you are going to learn through this book! So, let's move to the next Chapter and start learning!

QUICK CHAPTER SUMMARY

- Shortcuts are also called Hotkeys

- Their main benefit is that they save lots of time
- We are going to learn them by level

CHAPTER 2:

KNOW YOUR KEYBOARD

To begin this chapter, you need to recognize and observe your Keyboard deeply. The first thing you need to know is that there are 2 main operating systems in the Marketplace: Windows (by Microsoft) and iOS (by Apple).

The reason I'm telling you this, is because SOMETIMES the shortcuts will be different in each Operating System because the Keyboards are slightly different:

- iOS is used by MacBooks, and MacBooks have certain shortcuts
- Windows is used by lots of PC brands (Dell, HP, Sony, Toshiba, etc.), and those brands use another type of

shortcuts because the keyboard is different.

Before you move ahead, identify if the brand of your Computer. If it is an Apple, you will use the MacBook Shortcuts. If it is another brand, you will use the Windows Shortcuts.

THE MOST IMPORTANT KEYS IN YOUR KEYBOARD

For shortcuts, you will have some Keys that are used again and again. Those are the following:

WINDOWS PC:

The most used for excel shortcuts are CTRL, ALT, SHIFT AND TAB. Sometimes you will use Function (FN), but almost never.

By far, **the MOST Important one is CTRL (Control) when using Windows.**

Please identify those Keys in your Keyboard. **They are in the Bottom Left corner.**

Normal Windows (PC) Keyboard

APPLE MACBOOK:

The most used Keys for Excel shortcuts are COMMAND, ALT (also called

Option and sometimes it has this symbol ⌥),
CONTROL, SHIFT and TAB. As with
Windows, you will rarely use Function (FN).

Normal Mac (Apple) Keyboard

The MAIN BIG DIFFERENCE between Windows and Macbook (when talking about shortcuts) is that **in a MacBook the most important Key is COMMAND**, not Control.

Please identify those Keys in your Keyboard. **They are in the Bottom Left corner.**

IMPORTANT NOTES:

Sometimes the TAB key is shown like this:

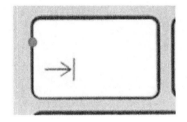

And the SHIFT key like this. (Don't get confused by the 2 arrows. The bottom one is the SHIFT, while the upper one is CAPS LOCK)

Now that you have identified your Keyboard and that you know the most important Keys we are going to be working with, it is time to start your journey to become and Excel Shortcuts Champion!

QUICK CHAPTER SUMMARY:

For Excel shortcuts, the most important Keys in your Keyboard are in the bottom left corner.

CHAPTER 3:

BASIC SHORTCUTS FOR ANY COMPUTER USER (LEVEL 0)

IMPORTANT NOTE: SHORTCUTS ARE ACTIVATED BY PRESSING <u>2 OR MORE KEYS AT THE SAME TIME.</u>

ALTHOUGH SOME TIMES YOU CAN RELEASE ONE OF THEM WHILE STILL PRESSING (HOLDING) THE OTHER IN ORDER TO CONTINUE TO EXECUTE THAT SHORTCUT

This is a super easy chapter but I just want to make sure that you understand these few shortcuts first because they are meant to be a way to maximize your speed while using a computer.

IMPORTANT NOTE:

I am aware that the shortcuts in this chapter may seem silly or kind of unnecessary (because you may already know them) but I just want to make sure that everyone who reads this book knows them. So, just take this Chapter (Level 0) as an introduction or as a foundation for what you are going to learn throughout the entire book.

SHORTCUT TO CHANGE BETWEEN INTERNET BROWSER TABS AND EXCEL SPREADSHEETS

WINDOWS: Ctrl + Tab

MAC: Ctrl + Tab

When you are using an Internet

Browser (like Google Chrome, Safari, Opera, Firefox, etc.) this shortcut will move you to the next Tab fast, from left to right.

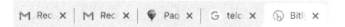

When using Excel, this shortcut will change between different Open (Active) Spreadsheets.

EXERCISE

Open your Internet Explorer (the one that you like most) and open 5 different Tabs or Websites

To move to the next TAB in your explorer without using the mouse, use this 1 step process:

Step 1: Press Ctrl and at the same time Press Tab, and finally release both keys. You will see that you are now in another TAB.

To move between MULTIPLE Tabs from

the left to the right, use this process instead:

Step 1: Press and **"hold"** Ctrl and at the same time Press Tab

Step 2: Release Tab WITHOUT RELEASING CTRL **(hold Ctrl)**

Step 3: Press Tab again

Step 4: Release Tab WITHOUT RELEASING CTRL

Step 5: Press Tab again

Notice that you are able to move between as many tabs as you want within you explorer.

IMPORTANT NOTE: In this Exercise you noticed the word "HOLD". Whenever is mandatory to keep pressing one Key in order for the Shortcut to work, I'm going to use the word "HOLD"

In the exercise above, it was Mandatory to keep pressing (HOLDING) the Key Ctrl

in order for the shortcut to work. While with the **Tab Key**, you could press and release (Tap) it as many times as you want.

To move between MULTIPLE Tabs from RIGHT TO LEFT, use this process instead:

Repeat the same process but with this shortcut:

Ctrl + Shift + Tab

You will need to "HOLD" Crtl and Shift, while "Tapping" the Tab Key.

EXERCISE

Open 3 Excel spreadsheets at the same time and try the following shortcut:

Ctrl + Tab

You will notice that you can change between those spreadsheets fast!

SHORTCUT TO CHANGE ANY OPEN WINDOW

WINDOWS: Alt + Tab

MAC: Alt + Tab

NOTE: Remember that in Mac, the ALT key is also called Option and sometimes it has this symbol ⌥

This one is simple, with this Shortcut you get to alternate between all the open windows. Even if you have 1 Excel, 2 Explorers, 3 Words, 1 Photoshop, with this shortcut you will move.

EXERCISE

Open multiple programs and try the shortcut Alt + Tab

SHORTCUT TO CHANGE BETWEEN

PROGRAMS

(JUST FOR MAC)

MAC: Command + Tab

With this shortcut you can change between Programs, not between open windows. In other words, you can change between Excel, Word, Google Chrome, Photoshop, etc.,

EXERCISE

Imagine that you have 2 Excel spreadsheets, 3 Word documents and 1 Internet Explorer (In fact, open those programs). Then perform the shortcut

Step 1: Press and **"hold"** Command and at the same time press Tab

Step 2: Release Tab WITHOUT RELEASING COMMAND **(hold Command)**

Step 3: Press Tab again

You'll notice that you can pick the program that you want to see.

"SAVE AS" SHORTCUT

TO SAVE AN EXCEL, WORD OR POWER POINT DOCUMENT FOR THE FIRST TIME

(OR TO CREATE A COPY OF IT)

WINDOWS: F12

MAC: Command+Shift+S

Note for Windows: If you are using a Laptop, you may need to use the Fn *Key in conjunction with* F12

With this shortcut you can save your current document for the first time. We now it as "Save as" because when you are going to save your document for the first time you need to give it a name.

Also, you can use this "Save as" to create a copy of your current document by Saving it with a different name. Buy you need to be careful, because once you save your document with a different name you will automatically start working in that new document (The one with the new name)

EXERCISE

Open a New Excel document and perform the shortcut to "Save As"

Step 1 for Windows: Press F12.

Note: If you are using a Laptop, you may need to use the Fn *Key in conjunction with* F12

Step 1 for Mac: Press Command+Shift+S

Step 2: Now you can save your document with the name you want

"SAVE" SHORTCUT

TO SAVE CHANGES IN AN EXCEL, WORD OR POWER POINT DOCUMENT THAT HAS ALREADY BEEN SAVED BEFORE

WINDOWS: Ctrl+S

MAC: Command+S

With this shortcut you can save the changes in your document. Is the fastest way to Save the advance you make on your work.

EXERCISE

Open the same document you saved in the previous shortcut, write anything in any cell and the Save the changes

Step 1 for Windows: Press Ctrl+S

Step 1 for Mac: Press Command+S

Notice how, if you close your document and open I again, you will see that the changes were saved with that shortcut

SHORTCUT TO PRINT

WINDOWS: Ctrl+P

MAC: Command+P

This is the last shortcut of this chapter (Level 0 Shortcuts). Basically, when you need to print the document you are working on, just perform this shortcut and Excel, Word or Power Point will show to you the Print Display.

EXERCISE

Open the same document you saved in the previous shortcut, and perform the shortcut to Print.

Step 1 for Windows: Press Ctrl+P

Step 1 for Mac: Press Command+P

Notice how you were shown the Print Display, so now you can print faster any document without using the mouse.

That's It for this chapter, with these 5 shortcuts (6 if you are a Mac user) it will be incredibly faster to work in a computer. We haven't seen Excel shortcuts yet, but in the next chapter (Level 1) you'll learn a lot of them.

QUICK CHAPTER SUMMARY:

- The 5 shortcuts of this chapter (6 for Mac) are essential if you want to improve your productivity while using a computer
- 80% of the time that you can save OUTSIDE Excel, is going to be because of these 5 shortcuts (6 for Mac)

CHAPTER 4

BASIC AND MOST NEEDED EXCEL SHORTCUTS (LEVEL 1)

Here we are, Level 1 is all about Basic Shortcuts that:

- Are easy to learn
- Are frequently used
- Increase your productivity
- Contribute with 20% to 30% of all the time that you can save becoming an Excel Shortcuts Ninja.

And, by the way, **ANSWER KEYS ARE INCLUDED IN THE EXERCISE SPREADSHEETS**

Let's start now!

SHORTCUT TO COPY AND TO PASTE

WINDOWS and MAC to Copy: Ctrl + C

WINDOWS and MAC to Paste: Ctrl + V

Note: With this shortcut, for Mac you can also use Command instead of Control

I know this is a super basic one, but it is necessary to start explaining all of the following shortcuts and to start to build each shortcut upon each other.

The first shortcut Ctrl + C copies what is in one cell and the second shortcut Ctrl + V pastes the same text, formula and format into the cell that you want.

EXERCISE (Open Exercise Chapter4ex1.xlsx)

You will see the name of our heroes, and your job is to Copy each one of them individually and paste them in to the square to the right.

Superman

Spiderman

Aquaman

Batman

Step 1: Position yourself in Superman

Step 2: Press and Hold **Ctrl**, then Press **C** to copy, finally RELEASE BOTH keys

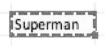

You'll notice that Superman is now surrounded by an intermittent square. That means that Excel has copied that cell and is waiting for you to do something else.

Step 3: Position yourself in the square next to Superman

Step 4: Press and Hold Ctrl, then Press V to Paste, finally RELEASE BOTH keys.

Step 5: Repeat the process with every one of the heroes

Superman	**Superman**
Spiderman	*Spiderman*
Aquaman	Aquaman

IMPORTANT THINGS TO NOTICE: You'll see that the TEXT was copied, but another important feature is that the FORMAT was copied also (The color and the type of writing)

EXERCISE (Open Exercise Chapter4ex2.xlsx)

Now you face an exercise where numbers are calculated automatically and you just need to Copy and Paste the Numbers in Bold (10 and 20) in each of the squares next to them.

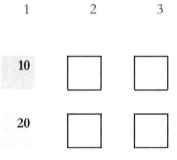

	1	2	3
	10		
	20		

Steps: Repeat the steps from the previous exercise

	1	2	3
	10	**20**	**30**
	20	**40**	**60**

Notice that the numbers change, Why? Because if you double click on any number, you'll notice that those cells contain FORMULAS.

So, when you Copy and Paste a cell that contains a formula, in fact, **you are COPYING AND PASTING THE FORMULA ITSELF.** That's the reason why you got different numbers, because 10 was multiplied by 1, by 2 and by 3. And it was the same with 20.

SHORTCUT TO CUT

WINDOWS and MAC to Cut: Ctrl + X

Note: With this shortcut, for Mac you can also use Command instead of Control

This shortcut is kind of similar to the Copy and Paste one. The main purpose of CUT is to Copy one cell, paste it on another cell AND AT THE SAME TIME REMOVE THE INFO FROM THE PREVIOUS CELL. That's the main difference.

So, while with Copy and Paste you would have 2 Superman, with Cut and Paste you will have just 1 Superman in the latter cell.

EXERCISE (Open Exercise Chapter4ex3.xlsx)

You will see again the name of our heroes, and your job is to Cut each one of them individually and paste them in to the square to the right.

Superman

Spiderman

Aquaman

Batman

Step 1: Position yourself in Superman

Step 2: Press and Hold **Ctrl**, then Press **X** to cut, finally RELEASE BOTH keys

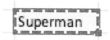

Step 3: Position yourself in the square next to Superman

Step 4: Press and Hold **Ctrl**, then Press **V** to Paste, finally RELEASE BOTH keys.

Step 5: Repeat the process with every one of the heroes

Superman

Spiderman

Aquaman

Batman

That's it! Now you know the difference between Copy + Paste and Cut + Paste!

SHORTCUT TO UNDO AND REDO THE LAST ACTION

WINDOWS and MAC to UNDO: Ctrl + Z

WINDOWS and MAC to REDO: Ctrl + Y

Note: With this shortcut, for Mac you can also use Command instead of Control

These 2 shortcuts are used to correct mistakes that we accidentally make.

With UNDO SHORTCUT Ctrl + Z you can go one step backward if you accidentally wrote or did something wrong

With REDO SHORTCUT Ctrl + Y you can go one step ahead if you accidentally erased something or did something wrong.

EXERCISE (Open Exercise Chapter4ex3.xlsx)

For you to understand this better, let's use our same heroes again. Your job is to Cut and Paste each hero ONE BY ONE in the right square, and after that you need to go backwards as if you made a mistake that you want to correct.

Superman

Spiderman

Aquaman

Batman

Step 1: Cut and Paste each hero ONE BY ONE as you did with the previous exercise.

Step 2: Once you have all your heroes in the right side, press and Hold **Ctrl**, then Tap **Z** two TIMES to UNDO TWO ACTIONS, finally RELEASE BOTH keys

Superman

Spiderman

Aquaman

Batman

Notice that when you pressed Z key one time, Batman went back, and when you tapped Z the second time Aquaman went back. Why? That's because each time you tap Z is equivalent to 1 action that you want to UNDO

Step 3: Now let's REDO the actions. Press and Hold **Ctrl**, then Tap **Y** two TIMES to REDO TWO ACTIONS, finally RELEASE BOTH keys

Superman

Spiderman

Aquaman

Batman

Notice that when you pressed **Y** key one time, Aquaman went back to the right side, and when you tapped **Y** the second time Batman went back. Why? That's because each time you tap **Y** is equivalent to 1 action that you want to REDO.

That's how you can use this pair of shortcuts!

SHORTCUT TO BOLD, ITALIC AND UNDERLINE

	WINDOWS	MAC
BOLD	Ctrl + B	Command + B
UNDERLINE	Ctrl + U	Command + U
ITALIC	Ctrl + I	Command + I

These shortcuts are widely used to format the cells, and they are going to make you

43

more productive in case you haven't used before.

Basically, they change any text like the following:

Bold Example

<u>Underline Example</u>

Italic Example

And you can also use 2 or 3 of them at the same time:

Bold and Italic Example

<u>*Underline and Italic Example*</u>

<u>***Bold, Underline and Italic Example***</u>

Let's start the exercise

EXERCISE (Open Exercise Chapter4ex4.xlsx)

You have a Grid, and you need to

format it with the Horizontal and Vertical formats there.

As an example, Goku will always need to be in BOLD (because the first column states that). So, in B3 you need to change Goku to BOLD format.

Then, in C3 you need the same BOLD Goku and additionally you need to UNDERLINE him. How? Copy and Paste, B3 to C3, and then UNDERLINE.

	Normal	Italic	Underline	Bold
Bold	Goku			
Underline	James Bond			
Italic	Iron Man			

Step 1: Make Goku in B2 BOLD with Ctrl + B or Command + B

	Normal
Bold	**Goku**

Step 2: Copy B3 and Paste it in C3 (Ctrl + C and Ctrl + V)

	Normal	Italic
Bold	**Goku**	**Goku**

Step 3: Make ITALIC Goku with Ctrl + I or Command + I

	Normal	Italic
Bold	**Goku**	***Goku***

Step 4: Repeat the process to fill the table with the correct Formats

	Normal	Italic	Underline	Bold
Bold	**Goku**	***Goku***	**<u>Goku</u>**	**Goku**
Underline	<u>James Bond</u>	*<u>James Bond</u>*	<u>James Bond</u>	**<u>James Bond</u>**
Italic	*Iron Man*	*Iron Man*	*<u>Iron Man</u>*	***Iron Man***

That's how you can format any cell in
Excel! Let's move to the next set of shortcuts!

SHORTCUT TO ALIGN TEXT

	WINDOWS	MAC
ALIGN CENTER	Alt+H and AC	Command + E
ALIGN LEFT	Alt+H and AL	Command + L
LOTS OF FORMATS	Alt+H	

Let's start with the Align Shortcuts. As
you can see, we are going to focus in the 2
most important: Center y Left

But also, for Windows users there is a
special shortcut that allows you to use key
combinations to access to the Ribbon without
using the mouse. That shortcut is Alt+H (and
its only for Windows)

Basically, with **Alt+H** you gain access to the Home Tab in your Ribbon

And when you press **Alt+H** you can use:

- **Alt+C** to align Center
- **Alt+L** to align Left
- **Alt+R** to align Right
- Etc

With that said, let's start the exercise

EXERCISE (Open Exercise Chapter4ex5.xlsx)

You have 3 grids and you need to fill them. You need to copy the names and paste them in to the next set of empty spaces, and then perform the shortcuts to meet the instructions (Center bold, Left bold, Center italic, Left Italic, etc)

Notice that you will have to use the shortcuts that you learned before (Copy, Paste, Bold, Italic, Underline)

CENTER BOLD		LEFT BOLD
Goku		
James Bond		
Iron Man		

CENTER ITALIC		LEFT ITALIC
Goku		
James Bond		
Iron Man		

CENTER UNDERLINED		LEFT UNDERLINED
Goku		

James Bond		
Iron Man		

Step 1: Copy and Paste the first set of 3 heroes (ONE BY ONE because you need to practice)

CENTER BOLD LEFT BOLD

Goku	Goku	
James Bond	James Bond	
Iron Man	Iron Man	

Step 2 for Windows: Alt+H and then A+C to center. When you are done use also the shortcut to make it bold (you already know that one). ONE BY ONE

Step 2 for Mac: Command+E to center and use also the shortcut to make it bold (you already know that one). ONE BY ONE

CENTER BOLD LEFT BOLD

Goku	**Goku**	
James Bond	**James Bond**	
Iron Man	**Iron Man**	

Step 3: Copy the set of 2 heroes (The ones that you aligned to the center) and paste them in the next empty Cells. ONE BY ONE

CENTER BOLD LEFT BOLD

Goku	**Goku**	**Goku**
James Bond	**James Bond**	**James Bond**
Iron Man	**Iron Man**	**Iron Man**

Step 4 for Mac: Command+L to align left and use also the shortcut to make it bold (you already know that one)

Step 4 for Windows: Alt+H and then A+L to align leftr. When you are done use also the shortcut to make it bold (you already know that one)

CENTER BOLD LEFT BOLD

Goku	**Goku**	**Goku**
James Bond	**James Bond**	**James Bond**
Iron Man	**Iron Man**	**Iron Man**

Step 5: Repeat the process with the remaining part of the exercise.

CENTER BOLD   LEFT BOLD

Goku	**Goku**	**Goku**
James Bond	**James Bond**	**James Bond**
Iron Man	**Iron Man**	**Iron Man**

CENTER ITALIC   LEFT ITALIC

Goku	*Goku*	*Goku*
James Bond	*James Bond*	*James Bond*

| Iron Man | *Iron Man* | *Iron Man* |

	CENTER UNDERLINED	LEFT UNDERLINED
Goku	<u>Goku</u>	<u>Goku</u>
James Bond	<u>James Bond</u>	<u>James Bond</u>
Iron Man	<u>Iron Man</u>	<u>Iron Man</u>

That's how you use shortcuts to align text! Let's continue, you are getting better and faster with each new shortcut!

SHORTCUT TO AUTOSUM

WINDOWS: Alt+=

MAC: Command+Shift+T

This shortcut needs no explanation. With this one you can Sum automatically any range of numbers without having to write the formula manually.

You can also get many results at the same time making this formula more appealing.

IMPORTANT FACT ABOUT THIS ONE: The place where the result (or results) appears (appear) will be determined by 2 important things:

1) The shape of the range of numbers that you want to sum
2) The cells that you select before using the Autosum shortcut or the cell you are positioned in when you use the shortcut

Because of that, in the following exercise I'm going to use **YELLOW COLORED HIGHLIGHTED CELLS TO INDICATE TO YOU WHICH CELLS YOU NEED TO SELECT,** so you can see the difference between different selections.

EXERCISE (Open Exercise Chapter4ex6.xlsx)

You have a lot of numbers to Sum! Use the yellow colored highlighted areas to select those areas and then perform the shortcut. See what happens and notice where the result appears.

Let's start with Exercise A

EXERCISE A

6

9

8

4

3

☐

Step 1: You have 2 options:

Option 1: Select the YELLOW area

Option 2: Position yourself in the

square bellow the yellow area (Cell B9)

Both options will get to the same result.

Step 2 for Windows: Alt+= to Autosum

Step 2 for Mac: Command+Shift+T to Autosum

EXERCISE A

6

9

8

4

3

30

That's it, with that kind of "Numbers shape" you will get the result below them.

Now, let's start with Exercise B

EXERCISE B

8	6	8	3	

Step 1: You have the same 2 options:

Option 1: Select the YELLOW area

Option 2: Position yourself in the square bellow the yellow area (Cell J5)

Step 2: Use the shortcut

EXERCISE B

8	6	8	3	25

With that kind of "Numbers shape" you will get the result to the right of the numbers.

Now, let's start with Exercise C

EXERCISE C

10	5
7	5
3	2
1	7

Step 1: You have the same 2 options:

Option 1: Select the YELLOW area

Option 2: Select the 2 squares bellow the yellow area (Cells B17 and C17 at the same time)

Step 2: Use the shortcut

EXERCISE C

10	5
7	5
3	2
1	7

	21	19

With that kind of "Numbers shape" you will get 2 results, one below each column.

Now, let's start with Exercise D

EXERCISE D

8	2	4	5
8	3	5	6

Step 1: You have the same 2 options, but this time use the option 1.

Option 1: Select the YELLOW area

Step 2: Use the shortcut

EXERCISE D

8	2	4	5
8	3	5	6
16	5	9	11

Notice that it doesn't matter if the range is horizontal, you will get the results below each column. So, what can you do if you want the results to the right? Let's look at it with Exercise E.

Exercise E

EXERCISE E

1	7	2	4	
4	7	8	4	

Step 1: If you want the results to the right you have 2 options.

Option 1: Select the YELLOW area, INCLUDING THE CELLS TO THE

RIGHT WHERE YOU WANT THE RESULTS.

Option 2: Select the 2 Cells where you want the result (Cells F22 and F23)

Step 2: Use the shortcut

EXERCISE E

1	7	2	4	14
4	7	8	4	23

With that kind of "Numbers shape" you need to do that in order to get the results to the right.

Exercise F

EXERCISE F

8	5	2	6	
3	8	1	9	
8	8	3	1	

2	5	1	1	

What if you want results below and to the right at the same time?

Step 1: Select the YELLOW area, INCLÚDING THE CELLS TO THE RIGHT AND BELLOW WHERE YOU WANT THE RESULTS (and including the bottom right one)

Step 2: Use the shortcut

8	5	2	6	21
3	8	1	9	21
8	8	3	1	20
2	5	1	1	9
21	26	7	17	71

Notice that you get every sum at the same time, including the TOTAL SUM at the bottom right corner.

GREAT! I'm sure this shortcut will save lots of time for you. Let's keep moving!

SHORTCUT TO SELECT MULTIPLE SEPARATED CELLS

WINDOWS: Ctrl + Left Click

MAC: Command + Left Click

This shortcut is super useful. With it you can select the cells you want, normally to copy and paste them in other cells. The most important attribute that this shortcut has is that it allows you to select cells that separated (not contiguous) and paste them in contiguous cells.

EXERCISE (Open Exercise Chapter4ex7.xlsx)

You have one task, you need to copy

and paste the Justice League heroes (gray color) in the Yellow square below the word Justice League. Then repeat that process with Marvel heroes and Dragon Ball heroes.

This process is faster if you use the shortcut that you are learning now

	JUSTICE LEAGUE	MARVEL	DRAGON BALL
Batman			
Captain America			
Goku			
Aquaman			
Thor			
Gohan			
Wonder Woman			
Iron Man			
Flash			
Vegeta			

Step 1 for Windows: Hold Ctrl and then left click on Batman, Aquaman, Wonder Woman and Flash.

Step 1 for Mac: Hold Command and then left click on Batman, Aquaman, Wonder Woman and Flash.

IMPORTANT NOTE: If you don't want to hold Ctrl/Command the whole time, you can release it after each click, the important thing is that you hold Ctrl or Command right before you click the next name.

Notice how you selected non-contiguous cells.

Step 2: Use the shortcut to copy

Step 3: Use the shortcut to Paste in cell C4

JUSTICE LEAGUE	MARV EL	DRAGON BALL

Batman	Batman		
Captain America	Aquaman		
Goku	Wonder Woman		
Aquaman	Flash		
Thor			
Gohan			
Wonder Woman			
Iron Man			
Flash			
Vegeta			

Notice how the 4 heroes where pasted one below each other. That's how this shortcut works when you copy and paste non-contiguous cells.

Step 3: Do the same with Marvel and Dragon Ball heroes

	JUSTICE LEAGUE	MARVEL	DRAGON BALL
Batman	Batman	Captain America	Goku
Captain America	Aquaman	Thor	Gohan
Goku	Wonder Woman	Iron Man	Vegeta
Aquaman	Flash		
Thor			
Gohan			
Wonder Woman			
Iron Man			
Flash			
Vegeta			

That's it, now you know how to select separated cells at the same.

By the way, you can also format them (change color, change to bold, etc.) in the same form, you just need to select them using Ctrl or Command and then click on each cell. Try to do it too.

Instead of using the copy shortcut, use the Bold, Underline and Italic shortcuts.

Batman
Captain America
<u>Goku</u>
Aquaman
Thor
<u>Gohan</u>
Wonder Woman
Iron Man
Flash
<u>Vegeta</u>

SHORTCUT TO EDIT CELL

WINDOWS: F2 or Fn+F2 **if you are on a Laptop**

MAC: Ctrl+U or Fn+F2 **if you are on a Laptop**

This shortcut is used to edit a text or a formula inside a cell. Normally, you would need to Double click to edit the text or the formula. Another option is to click the cell and then go up to the ribbon to edit that, but it is easier to use this shortcut.

EXERCISE (Open Exercise Chapter4ex8.xlsx)

The task is to correct the text and the formulas from exercises A and B.

Let's start with exercise A.

EXERCISE A

Batma

Captain merica

Iro Man

Aquman

Tho

Step 1 for Windows: Position yourself in B2 (Batma) and use F2 or Fn+F2

Step 1 for Mac: Position yourself in B2 (Batma) and use Ctrl+U or Fn+F2

Notice how you are now able to edit that cell.

Step 2: Write the missing letter to have "Batman"

Step 3: Repeat the process with "Captain Mérica". After you have performed the shortcut, you are able to use the left and right arrows to move through the text. Finally do the same with all the heroes.

EXERCISE A

Batman

Captain America

Iron Man

Aquaman

Thor

Let's start with exercise B.

EXERCISE
B

10.0	10
#¡DIV/0!	20
#¡DIV/0!	30
2.5	40
#¡DIV/0!	50

Step 1: Position yourself in D2 and perform the shortcut

Notice how a formula appears =100/E2 That formula means that the result you will get is 100 divided by whatever number is in the cell E2 (in that case is 10). So, the result is 100/10=10

That result is correct so you have nothing rewrite there. Let's move to the next cell.

Step 2: Position yourself in D2 and perform the shortcut.

Notice how the formula is =100/D12 That formula gives an Error because cell D12 is empty. What you need to do is to transform the formula to =100/E3 (The cell to the right of the result)

Do it and press Enter. If you do the same for every cell (correcting the mistakes) you will get the following results.

EXERCISE
B

10.0	10
5.0	20

3.3	30
2.5	40
2.0	50

That is how you edit a cell fast without using the mouse.

SHORTCUT TO WRITE IN A NEW LINE BUT IN THE SAME CELL

WINDOWS: Alt+Enter

MAC: Ctrl+Alt+Enter

NOTE: Remember that in Mac, the ALT key is also called Option and sometimes it has this symbol ⌥

This shortcut is used when you have a very long text inside one cell. Sometimes you will want to take one part of the long text and put it below another part to create some kind of paragraph.

Instead of:

"Singleness of purpose is one of the chief essentials for…"

—John D. Rockefeller

You can have:

> "Singleness of purpose is one
> of the chief essentials for
> success in life."
> —John D. Rockefeller

EXERCISE **(Open** **Exercise** **Chapter4ex9.xlsx)**

The task is easy, create paragraphs like the example you saw before.

Let's start with the first one.

"Lost time is never found again." —Benjamin Franklin

Step 1: Perform the shortcut to Edit Cell that you learn the section before **(Fn+F2 or Ctrl+U)**

Step 2 for Windows: Position yourself after the word "never" and perform this shortcut **Alt+Enter**

Step 2 for Mac: Position yourself after the word "never" and perform this shortcut **Ctrl+Alt+Enter**

Now you have something like this

"Lost time is never
 found again." —Benjamin Franklin

Step 3: Repeat the process positioning yourself to the left of the name "Benjamin" and perform the shortcut again.

"Lost time is never
found again."
—Benjamin Franklin

That's it! That's how you create paragraphs.
Now do the same with the remaining quotes.

SHORTCUT TO HIDE AND SHOW THE RIBBON

WINDOWS: Ctrl+F1

MAC: Command+Alt+R

NOTE: Remember that in Mac, the ALT key is also called Option and sometimes it has this symbol ⌥

This may seem like a silly shortcut, but when you use it you will find it very useful in terms of work space.

The "Ribbon" in Excel is the upper part where you have all the buttons to change the type of letter, to change the cell color, to align text, etc.

You can hide (collapse) and show (expand) the Ribbon in Excel. That's useful when you are dealing with lots of data in the screen because hiding the Ribbon gives you another 4 rows of visibility.

EXERCISE   (Open   Exercise Chapter4ex10.xlsx)

You have a Database and your task is to Hide (Collapse) the Ribbon to know how it works. Also notice that by doing that, you have more space to work.

Step 1 for Windows: Hide the Ribbon using **Ctrl+F1**

Step 1 for Mac: Hide the Ribbon using

Command+Alt+R

Notice how the Ribbon is not there anymore.

Step 1 for Windows: Show the Ribbon again using **Ctrl+F1**

Step 1 for Mac: Show the Ribbon again using **Command+Alt+R**

That's it! This one was easy.

CONGRATULATIONS! YA HAVE COMPLETED LEVEL 1 SHORTCUTS!

FROM ALL THE TIME THAT YOU ARE ABLE TO SAVE USING SHORTCUTS, THE LEVEL 1 SHORTCUTS THAT YOU HAVE LEARNED WILL CONTRIBUTE WITH 20% TO 30% OF THAT TIME.

Let's move to the Level 2 Shortcuts!

Are you enjoying this book?

Do you think it's easy to understand?

Have the exercises helped you learn faster?

Without knowing your opinion, I won't know if the book has helped you to become a better Excel user.

You can share your thoughts with me by writing a Review

CHAPTER 5

THE MOST TIME-SAVING SHORTCUTS (LEVEL 2)

Level 2 Shortcuts are the best to become the productive Excel user that you want to be.

Just as an estimate, of all the time you can save with shortcuts, Level 2 shortcuts account for almost 50% of that time. The reason why this is true is because you are going to find yourself using them frequently and at the same time, if you choose not to use the shortcut it is going to be too time consuming.

Simply said, you are going to use them a lot and there is no fast way to perform the action without them.

Let's start right now with Level 2 Shortcuts!

SHORTCUT TO MOVE TO THE EDGES

(I ALSO CALL THIS ONE "SHORTCUT TO MOVE FAST THROUGH THE DATA IN THE SPREADSHEET")

WINDOWS: Ctrl+Arrow

MAC: Ctrl+Arrow

This is one of my favorites because it allows us to navigate fast through the spreadsheet and it is easy to use.

Basically, you can do two main things:

- You can move superfast to and EDGE of a group of cells
- And you can move superfast to the next cell that contains data, it doesn't

matter the quantity of empty cells in between, the only requirement is that you move UP, DOWN, RIGHT or LEFT.

Let's try an exercise for you to understand this better.

EXERCISE (Open Exercise Chapter5ex1.xlsx)

You have several exercises and I'm going to guide you through them. Remember that the shortcut is performed just by Holding **Ctrl** and by tapping any of the **Arrow Keys** (Up, Down, Left, Right)

Let's solve EXERCISE A

EXERCIS E A

	Captain		
1	America	Consumer Services	3449
2	Robin	Gas Utilities	7147

3	Captain Marvel	Information Technology	5824
4	Picollo	Specialty Chemicals	8207
5	Batman	Health Insurance	3879
6	The Rocketeer	Insurance Brokers	2566
7	Superman	Electrical Equipment	3922
8	Batwoman	Auto Parts Stores	3642

Step 1: Position yourself in the Number 1 (**Cell B3** colored with yellow).

Step 2: Press and Hold Ctrl and then press **RIGHT ARROW** one time. Notice how you moved fast to the right EDGE, and now you are positioned in the number 3449 (Cell E3)

Step 3: Press and Hold Ctrl and then press **DOWN ARROW** one time. Notice how you moved fast to the bottom EDGE, and now you are positioned in the number 3642 (Cell E10)

Step 4: Press and Hold **Ctrl** and then press **LEFT ARROW** one time. Notice how you moved fast to the left EDGE, and now you are positioned in the number 8 (Cell B10)

Step 5: Press and Hold **Ctrl** and then press **UP ARROW** one time. Notice how you moved fast to the upper EDGE again, and now you are positioned again in the number 1 (Cell B3)

That's how you can use this shortcut to move to the EDGES.

Let's solve EXERCISE B

EXERCISE B

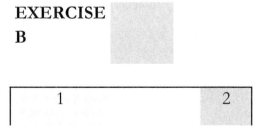

1	2

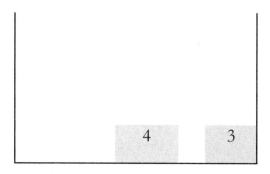

Step 1: Position yourself in the Number 1 (**Cell H3** colored with yellow).

Step 2: Press and Hold **Ctrl** and then press **RIGHT ARROW** one time. Notice how you moved fast through empty cells, and now you are positioned in the number 2 (Cell L3)

Step 3: Press and Hold **Ctrl** and then press **DOWN ARROW** one time. Notice how you moved fast through empty cells, and now you are positioned in the number 3 (Cell L7)

Step 4: Press and Hold **Ctrl** and then press **LEFT ARROW** one time. Notice how you moved fast through empty cells, and now you are positioned in the number 4 (Cell I7)

Step 5: Press and Hold Ctrl and then press **UP ARROW** one time. Notice how you moved fast and nothing stopped you of getting out of the box (because there was no full cell), and you ended in **Cell I1 (gray cell)** just because that's the top of the spreadsheet.

Step 2: Press and Hold Ctrl and then press **RIGHT ARROW** one more time. Notice how you are positioned in Column XFD1. That's the right end of the Spreadsheet!! To get back, just press **CTRL+LEFT ARROW**

So, with this shortcut you can move through empty cells also.

Let's solve EXERCISE C

EXERCISE C

	2

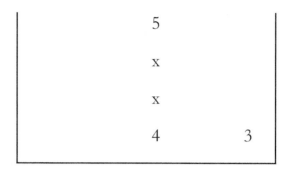

Step 1: Position yourself in the yellow empty cell (**Cell H16**) Now you are starting from an empty cell and moving through empty cells.

Step 2: Press and Hold **Ctrl** and then press **RIGHT ARROW** one time. Notice how you moved fast through empty cells and to the next full cell, which has a number 2.

Step 3: Complete the pattern by moving to number 3, 4 and 5.

That's how useful this shortcut is, and it gets better because (2 exercises ahead) we are going to combine this shortcut with another one. Let's continue!

SHORTCUT TO SELECT CONTIGUOUS CELLS

WINDOWS: Shift+Arrow

MAC: Shift+Arrow

This is one is used to extend a selection (one cell, one column or one row at a time).

Instead of using the mouse to select a small group of cells, you can use this shortcut and do it faster.

Let's try an exercise for you to understand this better.

EXERCISE (Open Exercise Chapter5ex2.xlsx)

You have a table with different colors, and your job is to select each group of colors, then copy and paste them outside the box (anywhere outside the box). But you are not allowed to use the mouse!

1	Captain America	Consumer Services	3449
2	Robin	Gas Utilities	7147
3	Captain Marvel	Information Technology	5824
4	Picollo	Specialty Chemicals	8207
5	Batman	Health Insurance	3879
6	The Rocketeer	Insurance Brokers	2566
7	Superman	Electrical Equipment	3922
8	Batwoman	Auto Parts Stores	3642

Step 1: Position yourself in the cell with the name of Captain America (**Cell C3**)

Step 2: Press and Hold Shift and them press LEFT ARROW one time. Notice how you selected Captain America AND ONE

CELL TO THE LEFT AND ALSO. Now just perform the shortcuts to copy, and paste that group outside the box.

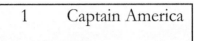

Step 3: By using the shortcut to MOVE TO THE EDGES (**Ctrl+Arrows**) position yourself fast in the number 8 (Cell B10). Then use the shortcut to select (Press and Hold **Shift** and then press **UP ARROW** multiple times until you have selected from number 8 to number 4).

Step 5: By using the shortcut to MOVE TO THE EDGES (**Ctrl+Arrows**)

position yourself fast in the CONSUMER SERVICES (Cell D3). Then use the shortcut to select: Press and Hold **Shift** and then press **DOWN ARROW** 4 times and **DOWN ARROW** 1 time.

Notice how every time you press the **RIGHT ARROW** one entire column is selected (4 rows and 1 entire column). That's how this shortcut works when selecting a range of cells.

Consumer Services	3449
Gas Utilities	7147
Information Technology	5824
Specialty Chemicals	8207

Step 5: By using the shortcut to MOVE TO THE EDGES (**Ctrl+Arrows**) position yourself fast in the name of BATMAN (Cell C7). Then use the shortcut to select: Press and Hold **Shift** and then press **RIGHT ARROW** 3 times and **DOWN**

ARROW 4 times.

Notice how every time you press the **DOWN ARROW** one entire row is selected (3 columns and 1 entire row). That's how this shortcut works.

Batman	Health Insurance	3879
The Rocketeer	Insurance Brokers	2566
Superman	Electrical Equipment	3922
Batwoman	Auto Parts Stores	3642

That's it! Let's merge those 2 shortcuts to create the next one. Let's move!

SHORTCUT TO SELECT LOTS OF DATA FAST

WINDOWS: Ctrl+Shift+Arrow

MAC: Ctrl+Shift+Arrow

This is one is the combination of the previous 2 shortcuts. You are going to use

Ctrl to move fast to the EDGE of a database and at the same time you are going to use Shift to select all the cells from the initial to the final position. Of course, you need to use the Arrows also.

EXERCISE (Open Exercise Chapter5ex3.xlsx)

Now you have a database (it is bigger in the exercise spreadsheet that in the book for space purposes). Your job is to cut and paste 3 groups of cells with the help of shortcuts. NO MOUSE ALLOWED.

ID	NAME	INDUSTRY	CITY
1	Captain America	Consumer Services	Toledo
2	Robin	Gas Utilities	Albuquerque
3	Captain Marvel	Technology	Denver
4	Picollo	Specialty Chemicals	Saint Paul
5	Batman	Health Insurance	Chula Vista
6	The Rocketeer	Insurance Brokers	St Louis

7	Superman	Electrical Equipment	Plano
8	Batwoman	Auto Parts Stores	Omaha
9	Hawkeye	Asset Management	Dallas

Step 1: Position yourself in the cell with the text ID (**Cell B2**)

Step 2: Press and Hold Ctrl+Shift and then press **RIGHT ARROW** one time. Notice how you selected in one single key stroke the cells ID, NAME, INDUSTRY and CITY (The entire row). That's the purpose of this shortcut.

Now simply perform the Cut Shortcut (Ctrl+X), Move to the yellow Cell labeled with "A" Letter (Using Ctrl+Arrow) and Paste the selection (Ctrl+V).

ID	NAME	INDUSTRY	CITY
B			

Let's move to the other group of cells.

Step 1: Position yourself in the cell with the number 1 (**Cell B3**)

Step 2: Press and Hold **Ctrl+Shift** and then press **DOWN ARROW** one time. Notice how you selected in one single key stroke the cells B3 to B31 (The entire column)

Now simply perform the Cut Shortcut (**Ctrl+X**), Move to the yellow Cell labeled with "B" Letter (Using **Ctrl+Arrow**) and Paste the selection (**Ctrl+V**).

ID	NAME	INDUSTRY	CITY
1			
2			
3			
4			

(Database will be bigger in the spreadsheet)

Let's move to the last group of cells.

Step 1: Position yourself in the cell with the name Captain America (**Cell C3**)

Step 2: Press and Hold **Ctrl+Shift** and then press **RIGHT ARROW** one time and then press **DOWN ARROW** one time. Notice how you selected all the remaining cells. (Te entire database)

Now simply perform the Cut Shortcut (**Ctrl+X**), Move to the yellow Cell labeled with "C" Letter (Using **Ctrl+Arrow**) and Paste the selection (**Ctrl+V**).

Captain America	Consumer Services	Toledo
Robin	Gas Utilities	Albuquerque
Captain Marvel	Technology	Denver
Picollo	Specialty Chemicals	Saint Paul

(Database will be bigger in the spreadsheet)

That's it! This is one of the most useful shortcuts because it enables you to select an entire row, an entire column, or an entire database in a matter of a second.

SHORTCUT TO SELECT CURRENT "REGION" OR "RANGE OF CELLS"

WINDOWS: Ctrl+A

MAC: Command+A

This shortcut is the fastest way to select a Database or a group of contiguous cells.

By performing this shortcut one time, you select the group of cells. By performing it twice, you select the entire worksheet!

EXERCISE (Open Exercise Chapter5ex4.xlsx)

You have a small database and an incomplete database. Your job is to Cut and Paste both in the "A" and "B" yellow Cells to the right.

Let's solve exercise A

ID	NAME	INDUSTRY	CITY	A
1	Captain America	Consumer Services	Toledo	

2	Robin	Gas Utilities	Albuquerque
3	Captain Marvel	Technology	Denver
4	Picollo	Specialty Chemicals	Saint Paul
5	Batman	Health Insurance	Chula Vista
6	The Rocketeer	Insurance Brokers	St Louis
7	Superman	Electrical Equipment	Plano
8	Batwoman	Auto Parts Stores	Omaha
9	Hawkeye	Asset Management	Dallas

Step 1: Position yourself in any cell within the data base

Step 2 for Windows: Press and Hold Ctrl and then press A one time. Notice how you selected in one single key stroke the entire database.

Step 2 for MAC: Press and Hold Command and then press A one time. Notice how you selected in one single key stroke the entire database.

(NOTE: If you do it twice, you will select the entire worksheet, but that only helps when you want to copy and paste an entire worksheet, so don't do it now)

Now simply perform the Cut Shortcut (Ctrl+X), Move to the yellow Cell labeled with "A" Letter (Using Ctrl+Arrow) and Paste the selection (Ctrl+V).

Let's continue with exercise B

ID	NAME	INDUSTRY	CITY
1	Captain America	Consumer Services	Toledo
2			
3			
4			

Step 1: Position yourself in any cell THAT CONTAINS TEXT within the data base. Avoid positioning yourself in an empty cell, because that would cause you to select the entire worksheet.

Step 2 for Windows: Press and Hold Ctrl and then press **A** one time. Notice how you selected in one single key stroke the entire database PLUS THE EMPTY CELL (In a sort of a rectangle)

Step 2 for MAC: Press and Hold Command and then press **A** one time. Notice how you selected in one single key stroke the entire database PLUS THE EMPTY CELL (In a sort of a rectangle)

Now simply perform the Cut Shortcut (Ctrl+X), Move to the yellow Cell labeled with "B" Letter (Using Ctrl+Arrow) and Paste the selection (Ctrl+V).

That's with this shortcut, is super easy and useful!

SHORTCUT TO MOVE TO THE NEXT OR TO THE PREVIOUS WORKSHEET

WINDOWS for next worksheet: Fn+Ctrl+Page Down

WINDOWS for previous worksheet: Fn+Ctrl+Page Up

MAC for next worksheet: Fn+Ctrl+Down Arrow

MAC for previous worksheet: Fn+Ctrl+Up Arrow

Note for Windows: If you are in a Desktop computer (with a full keyboard) probably you won't need to use Fn. But if you are working with a laptop-like keyboard, you will need to use Fn because you will notice that the Keys Pg Dn and Pg Up are in the Down and Up arrows inside a square.

Every time that something in your keyboard is INSIDE A SQUARE, it is going to be mandatory to use the Fn Key to activate that (apart from other keys that may be necessary also).

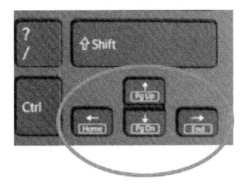

You will find the Arrow Keys and the Page Downs and Up Keys in the right part of your Keyboard.

This shortcut is the fastest way to move through the worksheets. Remember that the worksheets are the little tabs at the bottom of you Excel File.

Each worksheet may have different kind of information like:

- Suppliers
- Clients
- Sales (Daily, Monthly, Annually)
- Products

- Projects
- Payroll
- Financial Statements (Balance Sheet, Income Statement, Cashflow Statement, Key Financial Ratios)
- Etc.

By performing this shortcut, you can move through the worksheets with ease. This one is going to save lots of time because moving through worksheets is and action that is done very frequently.

EXERCISE (Open Exercise Chapter5ex5.xlsx)

You 2 databases similar to the previous exercise, and your Job is to Copy and Paste the upper one in Worksheet 1 and the bottom one in Worksheet 2.

The aim of this exercise is to do it as fast as possible and with the fewer movements as possible. NO MOUSE

ALLOWED.

Step 1: Position yourself in any cell of the upper database

Step 2 for Windows: Press and Hold Ctrl and then press A once to select the whole database

Step 2 for MAC: Press and Hold Command and then press A once to select the whole database

Step 3: Perform the Copy shortcut (Ctrl+C)

Step 4 for Windows: Press and Hold Fn+Ctrl and then press Page Down one time (if you are in a full keyboard maybe you won't need Fn). Notice how you changed the worksheet, now you are on Worksheet 1.

Step 4 for Mac: Press and Hold Fn+Ctrl and then press Down Arrow one time. Notice how you changed the worksheet, now you are on Worksheet 1.

paste here

Step 5: Now just perform the Paste Shortcut (Ctrl+V)

That's it! Now let's go back to the EXERCISE worksheet.

Step 6 for Windows: To go back, Press and Hold Fn+Ctrl and then press Page Up one time.

Step 6 for Mac: To go back, Press and Hold Fn+Ctrl and then press Up Arrow one time.

To complete the process (Paste the bottom database in Worksheet 2), **just repeat Steps 1 to 5.**

IMPORTANT NOTE: Every time you Tap PageDown/Up or UP/Down Arrow, is equivalent to moving 1 worksheet. If you want to move 2 worksheets, just tap PageDown/Up or the Arrows twice.

That's it! You have learned the fast way to navigate through worksheets in you Excel File without using the mouse!

SHORTCUT TO MOVE TO THE LAST/FIRST CELL IN THE WORKSHEET

WINDOWS for LAST cell: Fn+Ctrl+End

WINDOWS for FIRST cell: Fn+Ctrl+Home

MAC for LAST cell: Fn+Ctrl+Right Arrow

MAC for FIRST cell: Fn+Ctrl+Left Arrow

Same Note for Windows as the previous shortcut:

If you are in a Desktop computer (with a full keyboard) probably you won't need to use Fn. But if you are working with a laptop-like keyboard, you will need to use Fn because you will notice that the Keys End and Home are in the Right and Left arrows inside a square.

*Every time that something in your keyboard is INSIDE A SQUARE, it is going to be mandatory to use the **Fn** Key to activate that (apart from other keys that may be necessary also).*

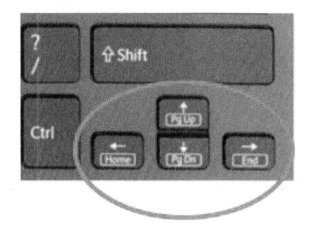

You will find the Arrow Keys and the End and Home Keys in the right part of your Keyboard.

This shortcut is the fastest way to move from anywhere you are to the last "active cell" or to the first "active cell" in the worksheet.

What is an "Active Cell"? Is a cell that has been edited. Even if you wrote something and erased it, that remains as an active cell.

What do you mean by "first" and "last"? The "first" cell will always be A1 because is the top left corner of the worksheet. The "last" cell will be the bottom right corner. You are going to see how this works in the exercise.

EXERCISE (Open Exercise Chapter5ex6.xlsx)

In this exercise you will find several worksheets. The purpose of this is that you move from anywhere to the "LAST" cell, and that, together, we discover the reason why Excel established that cell as the "Last" cell.

The shortcut is super easy to perform (just a navigating shortcut), but the important thing to consider is that you have some kind on idea of where you are going to land if you perform the shortcut.

Oh, one more thing, NO MOUSE

ALLOWED!

WORKSHEET 1

Step 1: Position yourself in anyone of the yellow cells

Step 2 for Windows: Press and Hold Fn+Ctrl and then press End one time (if you are in a full keyboard maybe you won't need Fn). Notice how you are now positioned in the last cell with the text DALLAS (Cell J14)

Step 2 for Mac: Press and Hold Fn+Ctrl and then press Right Arrow one time. Notice how you are now positioned in the last cell with the text DALLAS (Cell J14)

Step 3: Now, perform the same shortcut but backwards. Use the Left Arrow (or Home Key) to move to the first cell (A1).

That's how easy it is to move from the beginning to the end of a worksheet. It becomes even more handy when you have a big worksheet full of data.

WORKSHEET 2

Step 1: Position yourself in anyone of the yellow cells

Step 2: Perform the Shortcut to move to the LAST cell (the same as Step 2 in the previous Worksheet exercise)

Notice how you are now positioned in the last cell (CELL J16) **But, why is J16 the last cell?** Because:

- In the upper part of the spreadsheet you have a cell with the text "EXAMPLE" and that is the last "Active Cell" to the right.
- The last cell to the bottom is Kimbra Fuquay (Cell F16)

So, in short, the LAST ACTIVE CELL is the one that matches the last active cell to the right and the last active cell to the bottom. In this case, it is Column J and Row 16.

WORKSHEET 3

Step 1: Position yourself in anyone of the yellow cells

Step 2: Perform the Shortcut to move to the LAST cell (the same as Step 2 in the previous Worksheet exercise)

Notice how you are now positioned in the last cell (CELL F99) **But, why is F99 the last cell?** Because:

- In the bottom part of the spreadsheet you have a cell with the text "EXAMPLE" and that is the last "Active Cell" to the bottom.
- The last cell to the right is Herminia Kerfien (Cell F89)

Just as the last worksheet, the LAST ACTIVE CELL is the one that matches the last active cell to the right and the last active cell to the bottom. In this case, it is Column F and Row 99.

Great! In the next shortcut we are going to combine this one with Shift, making it a "Selection" Shortcut.

SHORTCUT TO <u>SELECT</u> FROM WHERE YOU ARE TO THE FIRST/LAST ACTIVE CELL

WINDOWS for **LAST** cell: Fn+Ctrl+Shift+End

WINDOWS for **FIRST** cell: Fn+Ctrl+Shift+Home

MAC for LAST cell: Fn+Ctrl+Shift+Right Arrow

MAC for FIRST cell: Fn+Ctrl+Shift+Left Arrow

NOTE: Same Note for Windows as the previous shortcut

This shortcut is a fancy way to select the cells from anywhere you are to the last "active cell" or to the first "active cell" in the worksheet. This way you create a "Selection Range" that you won't be able to create with any other shortcut.

It is easier if you look how it works while doing the exercise

EXERCISE (Open Exercise Chapter5ex7.xlsx)

In this exercise you will find several worksheets (similar to the previous exercise in order to make it understandable to you). The purpose of this is that you SELECT a RANGE of cells from anywhere you are to the "LAST" cell, and to the "FIRST" cell also.

WORKSHEET 1

Step 1: Position yourself in the red

square (D8)

Step 2 for Windows: Press and <u>Hold</u> **Fn+Ctrl+Shift** (I know it can be hard, but you can do it) and then press **End** one time (if you are in a full keyboard maybe you won't need **Fn**). Notice how you are now selecting the range of cells from D8 to Dallas (J14).

Step 2 for Mac: Press and Hold **Fn+Ctrl+Shift** (I know it can be hard, but you can do it) and then press **Right Arrow** one time. Notice how you are now selecting the range of cells from D8 to Dallas (J14).

Step 3: Now, position yourself in the yellow square (G7)

Step 4 for Windows: Press and <u>Hold</u> **Fn+Ctrl+Shift** and then press **Home** one time. Notice how you are now selecting the range of cells from G7 to A1

Step 4 for Mac: Press and Hold **Fn+Ctrl+Shift** and then press **Left Arrow** one time. Notice how you are now selecting the range of cells from G7 to A1.

This allows you to Copy, Cut, Paste, make Bold, Erase, or do whatever you want to do with the selected cells. That's the main benefit of this combined shortcut.

IMPORTANT NOTE 1:

IF YOU HOLD Fn+Ctrl+Shift **PRESS END (or RIGHT ARROW), Release the Arrow while holding** Fn+Ctrl+Shift **, AND THEN ALSO PRESS HOME (or LEFT ARROW), YOU WILL FIND THAT YOU ARE SELECTING ALL THE ACTIVE CELLS IN THE WORKSHEET.**

IN SIMPLE WORDS, PERFORM THE 2 SHORTCUTS AT THE SAME TIME AND YOU WILL BE ABLE TO SELECT ALL THE ACTIVE CELLS.

Now it is your turn to do the same with the Worksheets 2 and 3. Try it yourself and get comfortable using this shortcut.

SHORTCUT TO SEARCH A TEXT IN DIFFERENT CELLS OF THE SPREADSHEET

WINDOWS for FINDING: Ctrl+F

MAC for FINDING: Command+F

WINDOWS for NEXT MATCH: Shift+F4

MAC for NEXT MATCH: Command+G

WINDOWS for PREVIOUS MATCH: Ctrl+Shift+F4

MAC for PREVIOUS MATCH: Command+Shift+G

These pair of shortcuts are created to make your life easier when you are trying to find a word or a number in the whole Excel Spreadsheet!

The first one (to Find) opens a dialog box where you write what you want to find.

The second one (Next Match) finds the next equal text or number in the spreadsheet. When you arrive at the last value, it starts over again with the first one.

They are very useful shortcuts to learn, so let's try an exercise!

EXERCISE (Open Exercise Chapter5ex8.xlsx)

This time you have a big database with exam grades of our heroes. Your job is to find the ones with the following grades: 70, 80, and 90. Using the Find Shortcut and the Next Match Shortcut.

NAME	EXAM 1	EXAM 2	EXAM 3	EXAM 4
Captain America	65	77	92	70
Robin	80	65	88	87
Captain Marvel	53	98	96	54

Picollo	100	87	97	75
Batman	83	92	92	73

Step 1 for Windows: Position at the beginning of the spreadsheet A1 and perform the shortcut to activate the Find Dialog (**Ctrl+F**) and the write 70 inside the box and press Enter.

Step 1 for Mac: Position at the beginning of the spreadsheet A1 and perform the shortcut to activate the Find Dialog (**Command+F**) and the write 70 inside the box and press Enter.

Step 2: You'll find that the first match for 70 is Captain America in his Exam 4.

Step 3 for Windows: Then, perform the "Next Match" Shortcut to find the next 70 (**Shift+F4**). You'll notice that the next 70 is Hawkeye also in his 4th exam.

Note: To Find Previous Match just use Ctrl+Shift+F4

Step 3 for Mac: Then, perform the "Next Match" Shortcut to find the next 70 (**Command+G**). You'll notice that the next 70 is Hawkeye also in his 4th exam.

Note: To Find Previous Match just use Command + Shift + G

Step 4: Just do the same until you find every one with a 70. Then repeat the process to find the 80s and the 90s.

You'll find that there are six 70, four 80, and seven 90.

Additional Step: Try to find all the heroes with the word "man" in their names. You can do it by just performing the Find Shortcut and writing "man" inside of it.

That's how easy to find values and text within the spreadsheet!

SHORTCUT TO FIND AND REPLACE TEXT OR NUMBERS

WINDOWS for FINDING AND REPLACING: Ctrl+H

MAC for FINDING AND REPLACING: Ctrl+H

This shortcut is similar to the previous one, with the only difference that you get the ability to REPLACE the text or numbers that you are searching with another text or number that you want

By example, if in your spreadsheet you have a lot of cells that contains "Coca" and you want all of them to contain the full name "Coca-Cola", you can use this shortcut to replace all of the cells at once, fast.

Another example could be cells that contain "Mike" and you want all of them to have "Michael" instead, you can change them

EXERCISE (Open Exercise Chapter5ex9.xlsx)

This time you have the same big database with exam grades of our heroes. Your job is to Find and Replace the 95, 96, 97, 98 and 99 with an "A".

NAME	EXAM 1	EXAM 2	EXAM 3	EXAM 4
Captain America	65	77	92	70
Robin	80	65	88	87
Captain Marvel	53	98	96	54
Picollo	100	87	97	75
Batman	83	92	92	73

Step 1 for Windows and Mac: Position at the beginning of the spreadsheet A1 and perform the shortcut (**Ctrl+H**). You will be shown a dialog box, write 95 in the "Find" Section and also write "A" in the "Replace With section"

Step 2: Click the "Replace All" button, and that's it. All of the 95 will be transformed in "A".

Step 3: Repeat the process with numbers 96 to 99.

That's how easily you can Replace text and numbers in your spreadsheet!

SHORTCUT TO INSERT CURRENT DATE AND TIME

WINDOWS to INSERT DATE: Ctrl+;

MAC to INSERT DATE: Ctrl+;

IMPORTANT NOTE: If you are on a laptop, you may need to use Ctrl+Shift+; *because without pressing the Shift you normally are not able to access to the semicolon (;)*

WINDOWS to INSERT TIME: Ctrl+:

MAC to INSERT DATE: Command+:

IMPORTANT NOTE: If you are on a laptop, you may need to use Ctrl+Shift+: *or* Command+Shift+: *because without pressing the Shift you normally are not able to access to the colon (:)*

This shortcut is straightforward. You can either insert the current date with a shortcut or the current time with another shortcut. So, let's try it in an exercise.

EXERCISE (Open Exercise Chapter5ex9.xlsx)

The simple quest here is to insert the date and the time on the correct cells.

DATE HERE
TIME HERE

DATE

Step 1: Position yourself in "Date Here"

Step 2: Perform the shortcut **Ctrl+;**

Remember that if it doesn't work you may need to use **Ctrl+Shift+;**

Step 3: That's it, you have the date

12/06/20
TIME HERE

TIME

Step 1: Position yourself in "Time Here"

Step 2 for Windows: Perform the shortcut **Ctrl+:**

Remember that if it doesn't work you may need to use **Ctrl+Shift+:**

Step 2 for Mac: Perform the shortcut **Command+:**

Remember that if it doesn't work you may need to use **Command+Shift+:**

Step 3: That's it, you have the time

12/06/20
13:18

This one was easy. Let's move to another shortcut!

SHORTCUT TO ROTATE BETWEEN ABSOLUTE REFERENCES AND RELATIVE REFERENCES

WINDOWS: F4

MAC: Command+T

IMPORTANT NOTE for WINDOWS: If you are on a laptop, you may need to use Fn+F4 because without using Fn, the F4 key alone performs another action.

To explain this shortcut, it is necessary that you understand what an absolute reference is.

WHAT IS AND ABSOLUTE REFERENCE?

An Absolute References is used to "fix" or "immobilize" one part of the formula. It's super useful when you need to drag.

You have noticed from the previous exercises that every time you drag the formula, the cells within the formula are repositioned too. If you drag it one cell to the right, all the cells within the formula are moved one cell to the right.

Now let's suppose that you want that some cells within the formula remain the same, that's when you use absolute references.

HOW CAN YOU USE ABSOLUTE REFERENCES?

To explain this easy, when you add "$" signs to the cells in the formula (at the time of writing the formula) you are stablishing the absolute reference:

=A1*B1   Is NOT an absolute reference

=$A1*B1 is a Relative reference

=$A$1*B1 IS an absolute reference (you need two "$" signs per absolute reference)

With the absolute reference you are ordering excel that if you drag the formula, the first multiplication factor in the formula will always be A1.

With the relative reference you are ordering excel that if you drag the formula, the first multiplication factor in the formula will always be in Column A, but the Row will be moved in conjunction with the dragged formula.

In simple words, the dollar sign before the column fixes the column, and the dollar sign before the row number fixes the row.

Let's try with an exercise to understand this thing once and for all.

EXERCISE (Open file Chapter5ex11.xlsx)

Let's try to figure out the earnings

multiplying the hours worked by the hourly wage.

HOURLY WAGE	$15.00

HERO	HOURS	EARNINGS
The Atom	1349	
X-Men	640	
Asterix	585	
Maximus	1918	
Conan	1634	
Ethan Hunt	996	

Step 1: Position yourself in **C6** to write the formula (The Atom earnings) and write a simple multiplication formula.

=B3*B6

That way we get 1349 times $15.00 = $20,235

HOURLY WAGE	$15.00

HERO	HOURS	EARNINGS
The Atom	1349	$ 20,235

Everything is OK for now...

Step 2: DRAG THE FORMULA DOWN! And you'll see what happens.

HOURLY WAGE	$15.00

HERO	HOURS	EARNINGS
The Atom	1349	$ 20,235
X-Men	640	$ -
Asterix	585	#¡VALOR!
Maximus	1918	$ 2,587,382
Conan	1634	$ 1,045,760

Suddenly, you get $0 for X-Men, you get an ERROR for Asterix and you get wrong values for the following heroes. Everything is a mess!

What happened?

	HOURLY WAGE	$15.00	
3			
4			
5	**HERO**	**HOURS**	**EARNINGS**
6	The Atom	1349	$ 20,235
7	X-Men	640	$ -
8	Asterix	585	=B5*B8
9	Maximus	1918	$ 2,587,382

The formula was moved and now is performing B5*B8

	HOURLY WAGE	$15.00	
3			
4			
5	**HERO**	**HOURS**	**EARNINGS**
6	The Atom	1349	$ 20,235
7	X-Men	640	$ -
8	Asterix	585	#¡VALOR!
9	Maximus	1918	$ 2,587,382
10	Conan	1634	=B7*B10
11	Ethan Hunt	996	$ 582,660

The formula is performing B7*B8

The formula was moved because you dragged it! And now is calculating the values based on wrong cells.

What we really want is that the formula **ALWAYS** multiplies the **HOURLY WAGE,** we want to "Immobilize" that cell within the formula with **Absolute References.**

Step 3: Let's go back and fix this mess with the absolute references. Position yourself AGAIN in C6 (The first formula that you wrote) and ADD the Absolute Reference to the HOURLY WAGE.

HOW? WITH THE SHORTCUT!

For Windows: Double click in the cell, then click between the B and the 3, and Perform the shortcut or F4 for Windows. (Remember that you may need to use Fn+F4 if you are on a laptop)

For Mac: Double click in the cell, then click between the B and the 3, and Perform the shortcut or Command+T

IMPORTANT NOTE: If you perform the shortcut more times, you will notice how you can Rotate between ABSOLUTE REFERENCES and RELATIVE REFERENCES. That's the purpose of this shortcut.

$$=\$B\$3*B6$$

Now that you have the Absolute reference, you can drag the formula down!

HOURLY WAGE	$15.00

HERO	HOURS	EARNINGS
The Atom	1349	$ 20,235
X-Men	640	$ 9,600
Asterix	585	$ 8,775
Maximus	1918	$ 28,770
Conan	1634	$ 24,510
Ethan Hunt	996	$ 14,940

GREAT! You can see that everything is normal!

3	HOURLY WAGE	$15.00	
4			
5	HERO	HOURS	EARNINGS
6	The Atom	1349	$ 20,235
7	X-Men	640	=$B$3*B7

3	HOURLY WAGE	$15.00	
4			
5	**HERO**	**HOURS**	**EARNINGS**
6	The Atom	1349	$ 20,235
7	X-Men	640	$ 9,600
8	Asterix	585	$ 8,775
9	Maximus	1918	=$B$3*B9

Also, note that the formula ALWAYS uses B3 (The hourly wage) because you have immobilized it with Absolute References!

Now try to solve the following exercises by yourself!

145

1	2	3	4	5	6	7	8	9

987

1	

2	
3	
4	
5	
6	
7	
8	
9	

That is the way to use Absolute References. Sometimes they are not necessary, but sometimes you can't write a formula without using them, it will depend on the situation.

And that's the way this shortcut works. This time, the "Absolute Reference" explanation was harder than the shortcut itself, but it is ok because now you learned how to use them.

SHORTCUT TO ADD OR REMOVE FILTERS

WINDOWS: Ctrl+Shift+L

MAC: Command+Shift+F

This shortcut is used to Add or Remove filters within a database that you are working on.

Basically, when you don't have filters the shortcut adds them to all the columns in the database, and when you already have filters, the shortcut removes them from all of the columns.

One important aspect is that, if you have 2 or more databases in your spreadsheet with filters (and you perform the shortcut in a database without filters) the first thing the shortcut is going to do is to REMOVE the filters from the other database.

Let's look at the exercise.

EXERCISE (Open file Chapter5ex12.xlsx)

You have 2 worksheets (Exercise 1 and Exercise 2) and the purpose here is to learn to use the shortcut and see what it does in 2 different situations.

EXERCISE 1

HERO	HOURS	EARNINGS	
The Atom	1349	$	20,235
X-Men	640	$	9,600
Asterix	585	$	8,775
Maximus	1918	$	28,770
Conan	1634	$	24,510

Step 1: Position yourself in "HERO"

Step 2 for Windows: Perform the shortcut Ctrl+Shift+L

Step 2 for Mac: Perform the shortcut Command+Shift+F

Step 3: That's it, you have already

added the filters to all the columns in the database.

Step 4: To Erase the filters just perform the shortcut again.

EXERCISE 2

You have 2 Databases, one with filters (the right one) and one without filters (the left one). You need to add Filters to the LEFT data base.

HERO	HOURS	EARNINGS	HERO	HOURS	EARNINGS
The Atom	1349	$ 20,235	Zorro	1365	$ 20,475
X-Men	640	$ 9,600	Zatara	879	$ 13,185
Asterix	585	$ 8,775	Zatanna	1808	$ 27,120

Step 1: Position yourself in "HERO" from the LEFT database (Cell A2)

Step 2 for Windows: Perform the shortcut **Ctrl+Shift+L**

Step 2 for Mac: Perform the shortcut **Command+Shift+F**

Notice how this first time you perform the shortcut, It erases the filters from the right database, even though you are positioned in the left database.

Step 3 for Windows: Perform AGAIN the shortcut **Ctrl+Shift+L**

Step 3 for Mac: Perform AGAIN the shortcut **Command+Shift+F**

Step 4: That's it, now you have erased the filters from the right database and added filters to the left database.

SHORTCUT TO SELECT ROWS AND COLUMNS

WINDOWS and **Mac** to **Select Row:**
Shift+SpaceBar

WINDOWS and **Mac** to **Select Column:**
Ctrl+SpaceBar

Note: I couldn't use the Mac shortcut to Select Column in my Macbook Pro, so it is possible that Mac users have the same trouble. If this is you case, just click on the top of the column (Column letter) to select the column.

These shortcuts are going to be used as introduction to the next shortcuts. The purpose is to select fast the row or the column in which we are positioned.

As an Example, if we are in B3 and perform the "Select Column" Shortcut we will select the entire B column. And if we perform the "Select Row" Shortcut we would select the entire Row number 3.

EXERCISE (Open file Chapter5ex13.xlsx)

You have some databases, and your only task here is to position yourself in each yellow

Cell in order to perform both shortcuts to how they work.

HERO	HOURS	EARNINGS
The Atom	1349	$ 20,235
X-Men	640	$ 9,600
Asterix	585	$ 8,775

Step 1: Position yourself in "640" (Cell B4)

Step 2 for Windows: Perform the shortcut to select the Row **Shift+SpaceBar**

Step 2 for Mac: Perform the shortcut to select the Row **Shift+SpaceBar**

Notice how this time, the entire Row number 4 is selected

Step 1: Now position yourself in

"Krillin" (Cell A20)

Step 2 for Windows: Perform the shortcut to select the Column **Ctrl+SpaceBar**

Step 2 for Mac: Perform the shortcut to select the Column **Ctrl+SpaceBar**

Note: Remember that is possible that this one doesn't work on Mac.

Notice how you selected the Entire A Column.

That's it, with these shortcuts you are able to select rows and columns. **With the following shortcuts you will be able to Insert and Delete Rows and Columns THAT YOU PREVIOUSLY SELECTED.**

SHORTCUT TO INSERT AND DELETE ROWS AND COLUMNS

WINDOWS to INSERT: Ctrl+Shift+plus sign **(+)**

MAC to INSERT: Ctrl+Shift+equal sign **(=)**

WINDOWS to INSERT: Ctrl+minus sign **(-)**

MAC to INSERT: Command+minus sign **(-)**

These shortcuts are used to Insert or Delete previously selected Rows and Columns. They are very handy when you want to transform your spreadsheet, adding or removing space from them.

Let's look at the exercise.

EXERCISE (Open file Chapter5ex14.xlsx)

In this exercise you will have colorful databases, in order to explain how inserting and deleting works. The purpose is to apply the shortcuts to specific rows and columns to see what happens.

HERO	HOURS	EARNINGS	HERO	HOURS	EARNINGS
The Atom	1349	$ 20,235	Zorro	1365	$ 20,475
X-Men	640	$ 9,600	Zatara	879	$ 13,185

Asterix	585	$ 8,775		Zatanna	1808	$ 27,120
Maximus	1918	$ 28,770		Yoda	1035	$ 15,525
Conan	1634	$ 24,510		X-Men	640	$ 9,600
Ethan Hunt	996	$ 14,940		Vegeta	1812	$ 27,180
Tsunade	1103	$ 16,545		Wolverine	1869	$ 28,035
Aquaman	659	$ 9,885		Watchmen	1366	$ 20,490

INSERTING NEW COLUMNS:

Step 1: Position yourself in "1349" (Cell B2)

Step 2 for Windows: Perform the shortcut to select the Column **Ctrl+SpaceBar**

Step 2 for Mac: Perform the shortcut to select the Column **Ctrl+SpaceBar**

Note: Remember that is possible that this one doesn't work on Mac. If this is you case, just click on the top of the column (Column letter) to select the column.

Now you should have selected the Entire column B

Step 3 for Windows: Perform the shortcut Insert Ctrl+Shift+plus sign (+)

Step 3 for Mac: Perform the shortcut to Insert Ctrl+Shift+equal sign (=)

HERO		HOURS	EARNINGS
The Atom		1349	$ 20,235
X-Men		640	$ 9,600
Asterix		585	$ 8,775
Maximus		1918	$ 28,770
Conan		1634	$ 24,510

Notice how a NEW COLUMN was inserted TO THE LEFT of the original B column. Now, the original B column is the C column. Also notice that the Colors from column A were copied/replicated into the new column.

INSERTING NEW COLUMNS AGAIN:

Step 1: Position yourself in "$20,235" (Now is the Cell D2, because of the column inserted in the previous steps)

Step 2: Select the entire D Column

Step 3 for Windows: Perform the shortcut Insert Ctrl+Shift+plus sign **(+)**

Step 3 for Mac: Perform the shortcut to Insert Ctrl+Shift+equal sign **(=)**

HERO		HOURS		EARNINGS
The Atom		1349		$ 20,235
X-Men		640		$ 9,600
Asterix		585		$ 8,775
Maximus		1918		$ 28,770
Conan		1634		$ 24,510

Notice how a NEW COLUMN was inserted TO THE LEFT of the original D column. Also notice that the Colors from column C were copied/replicated into the new column.

INSERTING NEW ROWS:

Step 1: Position yourself in "Asterix" (Cell A5)

Step 2 for Windows: Perform the shortcut to select the Row Shift+SpaceBar

Step 2 for Mac: Perform the shortcut to select the Row Shift+SpaceBar

Now you have selected the entire Row number 5.

Step 3 for Windows: Perform the shortcut Insert Ctrl+Shift+plus sign **(+)**

Step 3 for Mac: Perform the shortcut to Insert Ctrl+Shift+equal sign **(=)**

HERO		HOURS		EARNINGS
The Atom		1349		$ 20,235

X-Men		640		$	9,600
Asterix		585		$	8,775
Maximus		1918		$	28,770

Notice how a NEW COLUMN was inserted ON THE TOP of the original Row 5. Also notice that the Colors from Row 4 were copied/replicated into the new column.

INSERTING NEW ROWS AGAIN:

Step 1: Position yourself in "Maximus" (Cell A7, because of the new row inserted in the previous steps)

Step 2 for Windows: Perform the shortcut to select the Row Shift+SpaceBar

Step 2 for Mac: Perform the shortcut to select the Row Shift+SpaceBar

Now you have selected the entire Row number 7.

Step 3 for Windows: Perform the shortcut Insert Ctrl+Shift+plus sign **(+)**

Step 3 for Mac: Perform the shortcut to Insert Ctrl+Shift+equal sign **(=)**

HERO		HOURS		EARNINGS
The Atom		1349		$ 20,235
X-Men		640		$ 9,600
Asterix		585		$ 8,775
Maximus		1918		$ 28,770

Notice how a NEW COLUMN was inserted ON THE TOP of the original Row 7. Also notice that the Colors from Row 6 were copied/replicated into the new column.

DELETING ROWS:

Step 1: Position yourself in "Aquaman"

(Cell A12, because of the changes we have already made to the original spreadsheet)

Tsunade		1103		$ 16,545
Aquaman		659		$ 9,885
Ben-Hur		1305		$ 19,575

Step 2 for Windows: Perform the shortcut to select the Row **Shift+SpaceBar**

Step 2 for Mac: Perform the shortcut to select the Row **Shift+SpaceBar**

Now you have selected the entire Row number 12

Step 3 for Windows: Perform the shortcut DELETE **Ctrl+minus sign (-)**

Step 3 for Mac: Perform the shortcut DELETE **Command+minus sign (-)**

Tsunade		1103		$ 16,545
Ben-Hur		1305		$ 19,575

The Aquaman Row disappeared.

DELETING COLUMNS:

Step 1: Position yourself in "1365" (Cell H3, because of the changes we have already made to the original spreadsheet)

HERO	HOURS	EARNINGS
Zorro	1365	$ 20,475
Zatara	879	$ 13,185

Step 2 for Windows: Perform the shortcut to select the Column Ctrl+SpaceBar

Step 2 for Mac: Perform the shortcut to select the Column Ctrl+SpaceBar

Note: Remember that is possible that this one

doesn't work on Mac. If this is you case, just click on the top of the column (Column letter) to select the column.

Now you have the entire H column selected.

Step 3 for Windows: Perform the shortcut DELETE Ctrl+minus sign **(-)**

Step 3 for Mac: Perform the shortcut DELETE Command+minus sign **(-)**

HERO	EARNINGS
Zorro	$ 20,475
Zatara	$ 13,185

The H column disappeared.

CONGRATULATIONS! THIS IS THE END OF LEVEL 2 SHORTCUTS! THERE WERE A LOT OF THEM AND YOU MAY NEED TO REVIEW THEM A FEW TIMES TO FULLY INTEGRATE THEM INTO YOUR

MIND.

In the next Chapter, we are going to go through the last group of shortcuts. Level 3 shortcuts are those ones that are not widely used, but they can save you big chunks of time every time you use them.

CHAPTER 6

EXTRA TIME-SAVING SHORTCUTS

You have made it to the Level 3, congratulations for that accomplishment. It is now time to learn the last few shortcuts of the book.

You may think that these are the most important ones, but that is not the case. The most time-saving shortcuts are the Level 2 ones, because of the frequency of use.

Level 3 shortcuts save some time, but they are not as frequently used as the Level 2. So, if you have to choose between learning Level 2 and Level 3, go for the level 2. And once you have mastered them, learn Level 3.

Let's start!

SHORTCUT TO HIDE and UNHIDE ROWS AND COLUMNS

WINDOWS and Mac to Hide Rows: Ctrl+9

WINDOWS and Mac to Hide Column: Ctrl+0

WINDOWS and Mac to Unide Rows: Ctrl+Shift+9

WINDOWS and Mac to Unhide Column: Ctrl+Shift+0

Note: The "Unihide" Shortcuts may not work in Mac. So, the only thing you have to do is to select both contiguous columns or rows, right-click inside the selection and click "Show" or "Unhide".

These shortcuts are used to manipulate rows and columns by hiding them. When you don't always need to see the information of a row or column, you can hide that one to have more space with other information you need.

EXERCISE (Open file Chapter6ex1.xlsx)

You have some colored databases and your task is to Hide and Unhide the following:

- Orange Column
- Blue Column
- Green Row
- Pink Row

HERO	HOURS	EARNINGS	HERO	HOURS	EARNINGS
The Atom	1349	$ 20,235	Zorro	1365	$ 20,475
X-Men	640	$ 9,600	Zatara	879	$ 13,185
Asterix	585	$ 8,775	Zatanna	1808	$ 27,120
Maximus	1918	$ 28,770	Yoda	1035	$ 15,525
Conan	1634	$ 24,510	X-Men	640	$ 9,600
Ethan Hunt	996	$ 14,940	Vegeta	1812	$ 27,180
Tsunade	1103	$ 16,545	Wolverine	1869	$ 28,035
Aquaman	659	$ 9,885	Watchmen	1366	$ 20,490

HIDING ROWS AND COLUMNS

Step 1: Position yourself in any cell from the orange column. Let's say you pick the one that has "1349" written (B3 Cell)

Step 2: Perform the shortcut to hide the column. Because you are on B3, Excel will now that the column that you want to hide is B column. Perform the shortcut **Ctrl+0** to hide the column.

HERO	EARNINGS
The Atom	$ 20,235
X-Men	$ 9,600
Asterix	$ 8,775
Maximus	$ 28,770

Notice how the columns was hidden. Now let's do it with the blue column.

Step 3: Position yourself in any cell from the blue column. Let's say you pick the one that has "879" written (F4 Cell)

Step 4: Perform the shortcut to hide the column. Because you are on F4, Excel will now that the column that you want to hide is F column. Perform the shortcut Ctrl+0 to hide the column.

HERO	EARNINGS
Zorro	$ 20,475
Zatara	$ 13,185
Zatanna	$ 27,120
Yoda	$ 15,525

Same thing, the column was hidden. Now let's do it with the rows.

Step 5: Position yourself in any cell from the GREEN ROW. Let's say you pick the one that has "Asterix" written (A5 Cell)

Step 6: Perform the shortcut to hide the column. Because you are on A5, Excel will now that the Row that you want to hide is row 5. Perform the shortcut Ctrl+9 to hide the row.

HERO	EARNINGS
The Atom	$ 20,235
X-Men	$ 9,600
Maximus	$ 28,770

The green row was hidden. And now let's do the same with the pink row.

Step 7: Position yourself in any cell from the GREEN ROW. Let's say you pick the one that has "Watchmen" written (E10 Cell)

Step 8: Perform the shortcut to hide the column. Because you are on E10, Excel will now that the Row that you want to hide is row 10. Perform the shortcut **Ctrl+9** to hide the row.

Vegeta	$ 27,180
Wolverine	$ 28,035

Wonder Woman	$	29,085
Tsunade	$	16,545

That's it. You have hidden Columns and Rows. But, how could you Unhide them?

UNHIDING ROWS AND COLUMNS NOTES

You will notice that in the middle of a hidden Column or Row, there is something like a thick line.

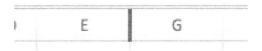

This means that the column F is hidden (between E and G obviously)

What you need to do is to select the contiguous Columns (In this example E and G) and then perform the Shortcut to Unhide the column

This means that the Row 5 is hidden (between 4 and 5 obviously)

What you need to do is to select the contiguous Rows (In this example 4 and 6) and then perform the Shortcut to Unhide the Row

UNHIDING COLUMNS

Step 1: First you have to select both contiguous Columns. To do that, just click on the letter E (the top of the E Column) and WITHOUTH RELEASING THE CLICK, drag it to column G to extend the selection.

D	E	G
	HERO	**EARNINGS**
	Zorro	$ 20,475
	Zatara	$ 13,185

Step 2: Perform the shortcut to unhide the column **Ctrl+Shift+0**

Note: Remember that on a Mac this may not work. Instead, you need to Right-click the selected columns and pick "Show" or "Unhide"

That's it, please do the same with the B columns that was hidden.

UNHIDING ROWS

Step 1: Just like the Columns example we did, first you have to select both contiguous Rows. To do that, just click on the Row 4 (the left of the Row 4) and WITHOUTH RELEASING THE CLICK, drag it to Row 6 to extend the selection.

3	The Atom	$	20,235
4	X-Men	$	9,600
6	Maximus	$	28,770
7	Conan	$	24.510

Step 2: Perform the shortcut to unhide the column **Ctrl+Shift+9**

Note: Remember that on a Mac this may not work. Instead, you need to Right-click the selected rows and pick "Show" or "Unhide"

That's it, please do the same with the Row 10 that was hidden.

That's how you hide and unhide columns and rows! A very handy shortcut, isn't it? Let's move forward.

SHORTCUT TO SHOW THE ACTIVE CELL IN THE SPREADSHEET

WINDOWS and Mac: Ctrl+Backspace **(The key to erase)**

This one is simple but useful in some cases when you are "lost" in your spreadsheet. The active cell is the cell that you are currently selecting.

Scenario 1: You see, there are some times when you are positioned in a cell that is not in the visible cells in your screen, but you don't want to move nor click anywhere else because the cell where you are is important at that moment. It just happened to you that you moved the screen anywhere else and now you don't know where your active cell is.

Scenario 2: You are not "lost" (you know exactly where your active cell is) but you are in other part of the spreadsheet and you want to go back to your active cell fast.

In both cases, the solution is this Shortcut because it returns the screen where your active cell is. Let's try a simple exercise.

EXERCISE (Open file Chapter6ex2.xlsx)

You have some colored databases and I'm going to ask you to position yourself in the yellow cells (G56 and E3) one at a time, go to the top of the screen, where you can't see the active cell, and perform the shortcut.

1850	$	27,750
659	$	9,885
1795	$	26,925
658	$	9,870

HERO	HOURS
Zorro	1365
Zatara	879
Zatanna	1808

Step 1: Position yourself in cell G56 with the number "$26,925"

Step 2: Go to the top of the spreadsheet (You must not be able to see your active cell)

Step 3: Perform the shortcut Ctrl+Backspace

Notice how your screen is automatically moved to where your active cell is.

Now, please repeat the process with cell E3 with the name "Zorro"

Step 1: Position yourself in cell E3 with the name "Zorro"

Step 2: Go to the bottom right of the spreadsheet as far as you can (You must not be able to see your active cell) even if you don't see any text.

Step 3: Perform the shortcut **Ctrl+Backspace**

Notice how your screen is automatically moved to where your active cell is.

That's how this easy shortcut can save a lot of time that otherwise you would have used to move through the spreadsheet finding your active cell.

SHORTCUT TO PASTE SAME TEXT, NUMBER OR FORMULA IN MULTIPLE CELLS AT THE SAME TIME

WINDOWS and Mac: Shortcut to Copy

WINDOWS and Mac: Shortcut to Select Non-Contiguous Cells

WINDOWS and Mac: Shortcut to Paste

This one is a combination of Shortcuts you already know, in order to create a more advanced shortcut.

With this combination you are able to copy one cell and paste it, at the same time, in multiple non-contiguous cells or in multiple contiguous cells

Let's start with the first exercise with non-contiguous cells.

EXERCISE (Open file Chapter6ex3.xlsx)

You have 4 different groups of cells, and

the word "Hero" is missing in 3 of them, your job is to paste the word in the 3 yellow spaces at the same time. In order to save time, you need to perform this combination of shortcuts.

HERO	HOURS	EARNINGS
Bumble bee	1035	$ 103,500

	HOURS	EARNINGS
Yoda	1054	$ 105,400

	HOURS	EARNINGS
Iron Man	1071	$ 107,100

	HOURS	EARNINGS
Legolas	1727	$ 172,700

Step 1: Position yourself in the word "Hero" (Cell A2)

Step 2: Perform the Copy Shortcut (You must know it by now)

Step 3: You will see dotted lines outside the cell with the word "Hero", when you see that, is time to perform the Shortcut to select multiple non-contiguous cells (**Ctrl+Click** in Windows and **Command+Click** in Mac)

What you need to do is to SELECT ALL THE YELLOW CELLS. Why? Because you are maintaining the Hero cell copied, and after that you are going to select all the locations where you want to paste the word "Hero"

Step 4: Perform the Paste shortcut

HERO	HOU RS	EARNI NGS
Bumble bee	1035	$ 103,500

HE RO	HOU RS	EARNI NGS
Yoda	1054	$ 105,400

HERO	HOURS	EARNINGS
Iron Man	1071	$ 107,100

HERO	HOURS	EARNINGS
Legolas	1727	$ 172,700

Notice how at the same time, the cell was copied in all those non-contiguous cells.

What happens when you need to copy and paste something in contiguous cells? Let's check that out in the next exercise

EXERCISE (Open file Chapter6ex4.xlsx)

This time, you have a blue cell (C4) with a formula to calculate the earnings (The formula has an absolute reference so it can use the $100 always). Your job is to fill the formula in the yellow cells without dragging the formula.

HERO	HOURS	EARNINGS
Yoda	1035	$ 103,500
Iron Fist	978	
Iron Man	1071	

Step 1: Position yourself in the word "$103,500" (Cell C4)

Step 2: Perform the Copy Shortcut

Step 3: You will see dotted lines outside the blue cell when you see that, is time to select all the yellow cells. Just select that range with the mouse as you would normally do it.

Step 4: Perform the Paste shortcut

HERO	HOURS	EARNINGS
Yoda	1035	$ 103,500
Iron Fist	978	$ 97,800
Iron Man	1071	$ 107,100

That's how you copy and paste Text, Formulas or Numbers in Multiple cells at the same time. Let's continue with the next shortcut!

SHORTCUT TO FILL/REPLICATE ANYTHING DOWN

(FORMULA, TEXT, NUMBER, FORMAT)

WINDOWS and Mac: Ctrl+D

This shortcut is kind of similar to the previous but it only works with contiguous cells that are below the one that you want to replicate.

In simple words, the main purpose of this shortcut is to REPLICATE the formulas, the text, the numbers and even the format of the cell that is on the top of you selected Range.

It's super useful when you need to fill fast your databases with formulas or repeated words.

Let's try an exercise.

EXERCISE (Open file Chapter6ex5.xlsx)

You have the same database that you had in the previous exercise, and a few examples more. Your job is to REPLICATE THE FORMULA in C4. And also, to replicate the word "Example" in F3 and the words "Another Example" in H3.

YOU NEED TO REPLICATE THEM in the yellow cells bellow them

HERO	HOURS	EARNINGS
Yoda	1035	$ 103,500
Iron Fist	978	
Iron Man	1071	
Watchmen	1366	

Step 1: Select the cell you want to replicate in conjunction with the yellow cells. The main rule here is that THE CELL YOU

WANT TO REPLICATE NEEDS TO BE
ON TOP OF THE RANGE YOU
SELECTED.

In this case, you need to select from C4 to
C15

Step 2: Perform the shortcut **Ctrl+D**
That's it, notice how you have replicated the
formula and even the format

HERO	HOURS	EARNINGS
Yoda	1035	$ 103,500
Iron Fist	978	$ 97,800
Iron Man	1071	$ 107,100

Now just do the same with the examples.
Select the ranges and Press **Ctrl+D**

EXAMPLE	ANOTHER EXAMPLE

EXAMPLE	*ANOTHER EXAMPLE*
EXAMPLE	*ANOTHER EXAMPLE*
EXAMPLE	*ANOTHER EXAMPLE*

Notice how you can replicate anything fast with this shortcut. Just remember that this REPLICATES everything DOWN, that's why you need to have the cell you want to replicate on Top of the selection range.

SHORTCUT TO FILL/REPLICATE ANYTHING TO THE RIGHT

(FORMULA, TEXT, NUMBER, FORMAT)

WINDOWS and Mac: Ctrl+R

This shortcut is almost the same as the previous one, with the only difference that this one REPLICATES ANYTHING TO

THE RIGHT.

The main rule here is that the cell you want to replicate needs to be to the left of your selected Range.

Let's try an exercise.

EXERCISE (Open file Chapter6ex6.xlsx)

You have the same database that you had in the previous exercise, and a few examples more. Your job is to REPLICATE THE FORMULA in D4. And also, to replicate the word "Example 1" in C7 and the words "Example 2" in C9.

YOU NEED TO REPLICATE THEM in the yellow cells to the right of them.

HERO	Yoda	Iron Fist	Iron Man	Watchmen
HOURS	1035	978	1071	1366
EARNINGS	$			

	103,500			

EXAMPLE 1

EXAMPLE 2

Step 1: Select the cell you want to replicate in conjunction with the yellow cells. The main rule here is that THE CELL YOU WANT TO REPLICATE NEEDS TO BE TO THE LEFT OF THE RANGE YOU SELECTED.

In this case, you need to select from D4 to O4

Step 2: Perform the shortcut **Ctrl+R** That's it, notice how you have replicated the formula and even the format

HERO	Yoda	Iron Fist	Iron Man
HOURS	1035	978	1071
EARNINGS	$ 103,500	$ 97,800	$ 107,100

Now just do the same with the examples. Select the ranges and Press **Ctrl+R**

EXAMPLE 1

EXAMPLE 2

EXAMPLE 1	**EXAMPLE 1**	**EXAMPLE 1**	**EXAMPLE 1**

EXAMPLE 2	*EXAMPLE 2*	*EXAMPLE 2*	*EXAMPLE 2*

Notice how you can replicate anything fast with this shortcut. Just remember that this REPLICATES everything TO THE RIGHT, that's why you need to have the cell you want to replicate to the LEFT of the selection range.

SHORTCUT TO INSERT A CHART

WINDOWS: Alt+F11

Mac: Fn+Alt+F11

Note for Windows: If you are on a Laptop, you may need to use Fn+Alt+F11

This shortcut is self-explanatory and it is the last Shortcut of the books! So, CONGRATULATIONS IF YOU MADE IT HERE.

With this shortcut, you can create a chart fast. Based on you selected data, Excel will automatically select the best type of chart an insert it in your spreadsheet.

Let's take a look at it with an exercise

EXERCISE (Open file Chapter6ex7.xlsx)

You have a database with the earnings of each hero. Your job is to create a chart just with 2 movements of your keyboard.

HERO	EARNINGS	
Optimus Prime	$	19,095
Naruto Uzumaki	$	14,175

Batgirl	$	23,415
Green Lantern	$	28,890

Step 1: You need to select the whole database, so the only thing you need to do is to perform the shortcut to select the whole range (**Ctrl+A** in Windows or **Command+A** in Mac). Now you have selected the whole database.

Step 2: Perform the shortcut to insert the chart **Fn+Alt+F11**

Note: In Windows you may (or may not) need to use the **Fn** *Key*

That's it! You now have a complete chart embedded there.

CONGRATULATIONS, YOU HAVE FINISHED THE BOOK AND NOW YOU ARE AN EXCEL SHORTCUTS NINJA!

I'm so glad that you learned all of those amazing time-saving shortcuts and I look forward to hear from you.

Please, share with me how you fell now that you can be more productive at your workplace!

How do you feel knowing that you can complete more tasks in less time and enjoy more time doing the thing that you really want to do?

I'll wait for your comments!

CHAPTER 7

QUICK FINAL TIPS

CONGRATULATIONS!! You finished the exercises and now you are an EXCEL SHORTCUTS NINJA! It was a great journey.

This book wouldn't be complete without a series of final recommendations that can help you even more

Here (in this short chapter) I can't teach you everything I'm going to recommend because they are extensive topics that would not fit in a few pages, it is also information that I teach deeply in other Excel books.

However, I want to make the following recommendations you with the hope that you recognize the main tools that you must learn to be an EXCEL NINJA.

WHY DO YOU NEED TO LEARN MORE FUNCTIONS?

There are hundreds of functions that can help you to better perform your work, however you may not know them. Sometimes a new function that you learn can save you hours of weekly work in the office.

The important thing to remember about functions is that they tend to relate to each other and become stronger tools when combined or in the form of nested formulas.

I'll give you an example you already know: VLOOKUP. The VLOOKUP function is quite strong and useful on its own, but when you learned to use IF together with VLOOKUP, three things happened:

1) You learned a new function: VLOOKUP

2) You learned a new function: IF

3) You learned a new tool: IF + VLOOKUP

When you learn just two functions you actually have three tools in your toolbox. That is, your tools are not just the number of functions you master, but also include the combinations you can make between those functions.

So, the more functions you know, the more combinations you can make and the more chances you have to become an Excel Champion.

That is why I created Excel Formulas Ninja! The purpose of Formulas Ninja is to teach you the TOP Formulas in Excel in an Easy and Fast Way!

Get your copy of Excel Formulas Ninja

"A STRAIGHTFORWARD, EXERCISE-BASED AND FAST WAY TO LEARN EXCEL FUNCTIONS" - *Employee from a State Department of Education*

"The book was engaging and encouraging by providing many examples and exercises. I will eagerly study the other books in the series."

"THIS NEW FORMULA MAKES IT EVEN EASIER THAN EXCEL VLOOKUP FUNCTION" - Manager of a Retail Chain Store

WHY DO YOU NEED TO LEARN KEYBOARD PIVOT TABLES?

Pivot Tables are the go-to tools for advanced data analysis! Whenever you are immersed in a gigantic amount of data and you need to take decisions based on that data, Pivot Tables are the way to go!

You can summarize thousands of rows and columns (literally thousands) in just a few seconds. You also can shape your summary to every imaginable way, in order to get relevant insight about your data.

Base your decisions in facts, not opinions!
Buy your Pivot Tables Champion

"THIS BOOK IS SO GREAT! NOW I CAN ANALYZE GIANT DATABASES WITHIN SECONDS!" - *Sales Coordinator of a Wholesale Company.*

WHY DO YOU NEED TO LEARN CONDITIONAL FORMATTING?

You will agree that the human eye identifies faster the colors and shapes than numbers. For the same reason, traffic lights have colors instead of numbers or words.

The conditional formatting in Excel is used to add colors or shapes when certain conditions are met, making the data user-friendly and giving the opportunity to recognize patterns within the data.

Imagine for a moment that you have a table with 100 data and you need to find the values that are closest to the average.

Option 1: The first option is to use the AVERAGE function and then manually search for those values within the table.

Option 2: The fastest and easiest option is to use Conditional Format so that Excel automatically colors the data that is closest to the average, and that's it, you'll have the data you need highlighted in the color you want in a few seconds, it doesn't matter if your table has 100, 1000 or 10000 numbers.

If you would like to search for the 10 highest values within a table, you can do so. If you would like to focus only on data that is less than the average, you can color them automatically. If you want to identify the data that are between 2 values, you can do it in less than 30 seconds.

That is why I recommend conditional formatting. Becoming a Conditional Formatting Champion will allow you to find the most relevant information.

Get your copy of Conditional Formatting Champion

"THIS GREAT AND EASY TO UNDERSTAND BOOK TEACHES A VERY USEFUL WAY TO ANALYZE DATA" - *Accounting Manager of a*

Sportswear Company

WHY DO YOU NEED TO LEARN TO USE CHARTS AND DASHBOARDS?

Charts are, by excellence, the way to communicate quantitative information in the business world, in non-profit organizations, in schools, in governmental organizations, in health areas, in sports, etc.

It's very simple, if you want to effectively communicate your numerical data, you need to master the Excel Charts. That includes the use of tables and the correct positioning of them, the selection of the data that you need, the Chart Type selection and the modification of the parameters of the chart.

Additionally, it becomes necessary that you learn to discover what a chart wants to "tell you". Correctly analyzing the data in a chart usually leads to better decisions.

If you want to make better decisions in your job or company, it is very likely that becoming an Excel Charts and Graphs Champion will benefit you

I WOULD LOVE TO READ YOUR COMMENTS

Before you go, I would like to tell you Thank You for buying my book. It is my wish that the information you obtained in **EXCEL SHORTCUT NINJA** helps you in your job or business, and that you can have greater productivity and more free time to use it in the activities that you like the most.

I realize that you could have chosen among several other Excel books but you chose **EXCEL SHORTCUT NINJA** and you invested your time and effort. I am honored to have the opportunity to help you.

I'd like to ask you a small favor. **<u>Could you take a minute or two and leave a Review of EXCEL SHORTCUT NINJA on Amazon?</u>**

This feedback will be very appreciated and will help me continue to write more courses that help you and a lot more people.

Share your comments with me and other readers

ABOUT THE AUTHOR

Henry E. Mejia is passionate about progress and goal achieving, he also loves to run and exercise. He works in the insurance industry and likes to invest in the stock market. While doing that, he devotes some time to create Excel written courses like this one, in order to help people to achieve their professional goals.

Henry also realized that the vast majority of people use a lot of their work time in front of the computer. That time could be used in more productive or more enjoyable activities, only if people knew how to use Excel a little better.

The goal of Henry's books is to open the door for workers and business owners to use Excel more efficiently, so they can have more and better growth opportunities, progress and free time.

Printed in Great Britain
by Amazon

77285191R00119